FACES OF
LAKE SUPERIOR

FACES OF LAKE SUPERIOR

By Dixie Franklin

Drawings by Carol Sutherby

A&M

Altwerger and Mandel Publishing Company

ISBN 1–878005–14–6 Cl
ISBN 1–878005–15–4 Pb

First Edition 1991

Designed by Mary Primeau

CONTENTS

PREFACE

IN THE NORTHERN FORESTS, hills and mountains where snows fall deep and summer briefly kisses the winter away, lies an awesome body of water too wide to see across, an inland sea with tidelike seiches between rugged cliffs and beaches of squeaky sand, a sea without the smell of sea. On some still mornings it is a mirrored sea which can turn awesome in her fury with wind-tossed waves and howling blizzards.

The first time I saw Lake Superior, I cried. Her beauty overwhelmed me, bringing tears to my eyes to stream down my cheeks until a kind breeze brushed them gently away. I seek her shores to vent my rages, whisper happy secrets, beg solace for my soul. Sometimes she whispers back; sometimes she rages with a temperament that can break mighty ocean-going ships in half to hurl them carelessly toward the depths. Yet I love this temperamental lake like no other.

Along Superior's 2,730 miles of shoreline which weaves a summer ribbon of blue against green forested borders of Michigan's Upper Peninsula, Wisconsin, Minnesota, and

Canada's Ontario, live a unique people. Their heritage is serenity of the heart, with a vision of white-tipped waves on the horizon, blue skies overhead and moss-covered woodland paths to soften times and an environment that could try the spirits of people carved from a lesser mettle. Her people never leave the queen of the inland seas for long; there are fishermen, professors, lumberjacks, storekeepers, politicians, bush pilots, trainmen, people with a tenacious and crusty spirit who live as they believe life should be lived, with time to stroll Superior's beaches to the heartbeat roar of waves, spray soft upon the skin and the sweet taste of freshness in the air.

As I roamed the Superior shoreline, I listened to their stories, their joys and sorrows, and above all, their love and respect for the mother of the Great Lakes. I wrote the stories as my tithe to the lake. One can almost see their faces in the waves, the trees and clouds: fisherman Hilmer Aakvik, who bought a fishing license every year until he died and kept his boat moored and ready at the docks; Bess Capagrossa, waking every morning with Superior through the trees; Rusty Hellman, beating out the rhythm of the waves with spoons.

I pass them on to you.

1

BUSH

CANADA'S BUSH COUNTRY gets to you.

It got to me again as I headed north on Highway 17 squeezed between a big Canadian and a pile of camping gear. I remembered all the nights when some restless dream floated through my open window to whisper half promises of canoes plunging down Algoma rivers, of moose peering through myopic eyes, of frosty mornings beside some broad-shouldered giant who loves the bush as much as life itself.

We turned onto the Chapleau road just short of Wawa. Rivers leaped from breaks in the towering spruce, peekaboo streams that squirmed underneath the road to disappear in a rush of bubbles. Boulders held deep-blue lakes in check, teasing my backward glance across intervening swamp.

Overhead, the sky borrowed blue from the lakes, white clouds dangling like baubles or long balloons drifting with the wind. Early winter sky.

With destination unplanned and only a restless thought on our minds, we took to moose country in search of the perfect

river that lodges in every hunter's dream. We found it on the Jackpine.

It shouldn't have been that easy. Perhaps the river was trying to make up for the time before the road went through, when the bush concealed the squealer's body from authorities until too late for the trial. The victim had reported poachers, then disappeared. Authorities finally found him deep in the bush, sprawled on the banks of the lonesome Jackpine with a bullet through his neck.

We stopped beside a low waterfall, slipped our canoe into the shallows and paddled off against the current. Alder crowded the banks to watch our passing. Patches of blueberries blazed crimson on the hillside. Graceful gold tamarack interrupted the green symmetry of the spruce and hemlock.

A mile upstream, the canoe skimmed through frothy patches of foaming bubbles unleashed from another stair-step falls. We made for shore.

When Canadians say *portage*, they bear down heavy on the last syllable until one envisions fur trappers of two hundred years ago with their laden voyageur canoes beached alongside. We portaged! Farther upriver, we climbed a moose-trod path to study the land. Finally, tempted by a warm boulder, I sprawled flat to listen for the heartbeat of the earth, to feel her prickly arms around my shoulders, to become one with boulders and the bush.

"See," I was tempted to call out to my friend. "You can't tell where I end and the bush begins!"

But he, too, lay sprawled from a nearby listening place. He apparently had some making-up to do with the bush himself.

Back at camp, we heaped a fire. As it crackled, a full moon reflected across the icy glaze which sneaked silently across the river and into our cove. At last, only glowing coals remained; the waterfall hammered out a lullaby.

Cold crept into our sleeping bags and huddled there beside us until the dawn. Old Man Winter had been busy. With icy fingers, he had sculpted white frosting over all the trees, scrub alders and wild rosebushes, sprinkling leftover ice particles across the river.

Mist rose ahead of our canoe as we broke ice to paddle through the pink of morning. With paddle dipping quietly, talking in low whispers, we eased around the last curve where the river opens up to make room for a long, skinny finger island.

There was a momentary freezing at the paddle. Then the hunter reached for the gun as the big hulking moose moved undisturbed through the icy bush. The boom echoed down the frosty channel to shatter the still of morning. The moose buckled. He rushed toward a far spit of beach, head erect. Boom! He whirled and disappeared.

We circled the island, searching for his exit, half hoping for a clean getaway. Four times around, and we found only the black smear where the moose had erased the frost on his way in. There was nothing left to do but search the swampy bog.

The hunter leaped ashore, pushed through the alders, and froze. A wide grin told the story of the thousand pounds of moose lying at his feet.

We knew the hunt was part of it—the hunt and the search and the final float back down the river in the overloaded canoe. But I suspect the big man was correct. The hunt was merely one more excuse for those born of the north to take to the bush and fall in love with this wild land all over again.

2

EVER THE FISHERMAN

MIST RISES SLOWLY from Frenchman's Pond which stretches its watery finger around the curve of river that ambles through jack pine forests. Puffy-cheeked chipmunks scurry along the pile of granite boulders, skidding to a stop to gather sunflower seeds strewn among the verdant mosses by a fisherman who frequents this place. A white-tailed buck saunters down a trail carpeted with fallen leaves. The ever wary animal lifts its antlered head to test the wind before slipping through the tag alders and willows that clamor for more growing room along the spongy shore. At the water's edge, the buck drinks its fill, then darts away. Moments pass and the pond is still again, mirroring the afternoon sun shadowed by white pine, spruce and tamarack. Suddenly a brook trout rises, triggering a succession of spreading ripples that sing their siren song to the fisherman waiting nearby, who has observed all that happened as only he can. The tall, gray-haired man rises eagerly from his resting place on a moss-covered root, reaches for his fly rod leaning against a tree trunk, then strides purposefully down the path toward the pond. It is a path he knows

well, having walked it for more than fifty years. Follow in his footsteps behind his rolling gait and enter the world of fisherman John Donaldson Voelker.

But be forewarned! Once you have entered John Voelker's world you will never again be quite the same, says CBS News correspondent Charles Kuralt. He calls his old friend the "greatest man" he met during his "On the Road" specials. Voelker's world is one of refreshing wonder, of discoveries as penetrating as a brisk morning wind, of ancient pines, pussy willows kissed by the last snowfall, summer sun and autumn gold. It is little-boy wonder spurred on by wanderings that may seem aimless but are as goal-oriented as a champ at bat, a teenager smitten by first love, or a nine-year-old heading for that favorite fishing hole.

"Fishermen have it even better than kids," Voelker chuckles. "Kids have only one Christmas to look forward to each year, but a fisherman has the same thrill of anticipation every time he takes off fishing."

It was as a boy that Voelker made his commitment to fishing, then arranged his world accordingly. He was the fisherman, ever the fisherman, even while lugging law books across the University of Michigan campus. He was the fisherman who served as prosecuting attorney for the county of Marquette; the fisherman who proudly donned the solemn robes of a Michigan Supreme Court justice for a period he fondly refers to as "my days in the black nightshirt"; the fisherman who wrote eleven books and saw one of them, *Anatomy of a Murder*, become a national best-seller and a memorable motion picture; the fisherman who, having done all those things, was never happier and more at peace than where he is now, home again, fishing.

Home for John Voelker is Michigan's rocky Upper Peninsula with its fabled trout waters, vast forests, meadows where white-tailed deer graze in the magical hours before sunset, wild mushrooms ripe for the picking, pussy willow, grasses and sugarplum. It is in this land, among these treasures, where the venerable judge forages with boyish delight.

Standing well over six feet, Voelker walks with the relaxed, measured motion of a man of the woods, his features chiseled peaceful by years of contentment found therein, his eyes, as blue as Lake Superior, watchful and perceptive of the smallest detail. With massive shoulders and rugged features, he bears a marked resemblance to the late John Wayne, a comparison he relishes with a wide grin. A creature of habit like the wildlife he so loves to observe, Voelker ventures forth each day in denim fishing jacket open at the neck, collar curled, cuffs unbuttoned at the wrist. Tan bush pants are part of his summer tuxedo of the north, bagging in the seat with one pant leg invariably snagged atop a sturdy camp boot. On his head he balances a flattened canvas hat, floppy brim, crown crushed flat.

One morning not so long ago his wife Grace cast an eye on him in his customary attire: "John, sometimes I think you try to look like a bum," she teased.

"Well, I am," he shot back impishly.

Bum? Can a fisherman be a bum if he never grows up? His back turned on convention, embracing a natural world free of pretense and phonies, Voelker thanks winter for sparing him from authentic bumhood: "Had I been able to fish for trout all year up here, I would have never written eleven books," he observes.

He strides jauntily down the path that circles his beloved Frenchman's Pond, watching ripples widen on the surface. At water's edge, he lifts his fly rod in practiced artistry, mimics the "aaanh, aaanh" whine of an unwinding reel, then sighs as his tiny fly settles delicately in the center of a ripple, all the while talking to both the trout and himself in quotable dialogue. Whether the trout responds is not the issue here: the maestro has taken up his baton, the fisherman is fishing the fly!

"It's like a dance. Ballet, not belly," he jokes, then adds somberly, "there are other game fish besides trout, but I admit it reluctantly."

He points out that trout are found only in beautiful places, a fact that draws him faithfully to moss-banked streams and quiet pools, which "give the waterlogged fisherman not so much the time and repose to think as, mercifully, the golden chances not to bother having to." Fly-fishing is the "quietest and quickest way to get out of town without attracting searching parties and baying hounds, while at the same time allowing the escaped angler to wander aimlessly for hours and sometimes days among the sylvan woods and waters he or she so loves without the risk of being labeled an amnesiac or strayed poet."

The judge is always happy to explain why he fishes the fly.

"I found that fly-fishing for wild native brook trout, compared to all other ways of courting these dappled mermaids, is oddly akin to the difference between seduction and rape." Voelker said it had dawned on him that in other forms of fishing, "the battle is virtually over when the poor deluded fish impales itself upon the bait, while here, when the beguiled trout responds and kisses the fly, the courtship has only begun with the outcome of the romance remaining always deliciously in doubt."

Voelker is as quotable as the books he has written, his sentences spoken as though they are to be, and may in fact already have been, set in type. It is as though he finds the correct assortment of words and phrases, writes them down and proceeds to quote verbatim from that day forward. As he speaks, the listener can never be sure if his comments are spur-of-the-moment "fifty-cent epigrams," or from one of his published works.

As he pursues the elusive trout, Voelker suspects that he is a frustrated ballet dancer at heart—"in my case an aging faun"—in squishy waders rather than tights. He further suspects that the rewards of fly-fishing may have less to do with the art of angling than with the art of living. "Being lucky enough to occasionally find oneself out there doing it [fishing] may be by far its greatest prize," he says.

He has never belonged to a fishing club, "except those of which I am the only member." And almost daily from opening day to closing, he is out there trying one more time: Frenchman's Pond or one of the other streams and lakes he has visited over the years, divulging their whereabouts only to trusted companions, scorning those fishermen who "kiss and tell." As he sees it, fishing is finding one's own place to fish, preferably a deep pool backed into the alders by a beaver dam or the rustling waters where a trout may lurk in the eddy of a waterfall.

Frenchman's Pond has become a legendary sanctuary for Voelker and those few fly fishermen and other confidants whom he occasionally invites to accompany him into this secluded corner of his world. He first laid eyes on the tranquil elbow of water more than fifty years ago while fishing with Carroll Rushton, a Marquette attorney and circuit judge who was at that time one of the few fly fishermen in the area. Later, Voelker purchased Frenchman's Pond and made it his special niche. He likes to fantasize about its past. Like a small boy, he imagines long-departed Indians stalking the game trails, or canoeing down the pond in the still of evening.

The pond has remained much the same throughout the years, save a scattering of fishing stands protruding along the water's edge, a concession to the spongy sphagnum shore. And the props:

one-room cabin with shingled roof containing mandatory cribbage board, assorted fishing gear, old bottles with their bouquets of wild grasses, and Old Fashioneds that appear every day at four P.M. or whenever the anglers-in-residence want it to be four P.M. On the outside above the door hangs a dinner bell to summon the tardy.

Feasts, Voelker-style, are often concocted on an oversized outdoor fireplace, with chef and longtime fishing pal Ted Bogdan doing the honors. Once fed, guests relax on weathered church pews perched on the boulders overlooking the pond.

Across a bridge and through the pines looms the skeleton of a tepee begun by a Menominee Indian friend who once spent time at the pond. Although its saplings never held the stretch of deerskin nor were warmed by a cooking fire, Voelker admires the tepee, a rugged tribute to an ancient skill. He treasures the poem that his Menominee friend Jim inscribed on birch bark and left hanging on the cabin wall, where it remains:

We walked here once, Grandfather.
These trees, ponds, these springs and streams,
And that big flat rock across the water over there.
We used to meet with you over there –
Remember, Grandfather?
But something happened, Grandfather.
We have lost our way somewhere and
Everything is going away.
The four-legged, the trees, spring and streams,
Even the big water where the Laughing Whitefish goes,
And the big sky of many eagles
Are saying goodbye.
Come back, Grandfather, come back.

Voelker said he "inherited the fishing sins" of his father, beginning his trout-fishing days not with artificial fly but with live bait, setting forth on bicycle, bamboo pole on his shoulder and bait can in hand, to conquer the nearest trout stream and return home to dump twenty or thirty trout in the kitchen sink.

"I guess I thought they were unlimited," he recalls.

Other things were also shaping the future of young Johnny Voelker: music, cigars, and his father's Negaunee saloon, which boasted the longest bar in the peninsula and attracted many of the characters whose dialects and other mannerisms have shown up in Voelker's books.

"I was born around the turn of the century, although lately I sometimes get turned around about precisely which century," Voelker laughs. He was born to George Oliver and Annie Isabella Traver Voelker in 1903, the youngest of six sons. In 1843, John's grandparents had emigrated from Effelder, Germany, with dreams of establishing a brewery in America. By train and boat they arrived in Sault Ste. Marie to discover the town already had its brewery. They pushed west across the Upper Peninsula by ox cart to Eagle River in the Keweenaw Peninsula, with an eye on the ready market for their product at Fort Wilkins and among local copper miners. John's grandfather followed the mines, establishing other breweries in Ontonagon and Negaunee. During prohibition, the Negaunee brewery was converted to a soda fountain, which male members of the Voelker family considered "a terrible comedown."

Voelker attributes his success as a writer to being "moderately literate" and reading a lot as a child. His first childhood story was entitled, "Lost All Night Alone in a Swamp with a Bear."

"Eleven books later, I am still trying to recapture that simple prose of saying everything I have to say in a single title," he said.

Thus were formed his most enduring passions—fishing and writing. In search of methods to pursue them, Voelker turned to the law, perhaps influenced by his sense of justice, romanticism, his devotion to detail, flair for the dramatic, and possibly the simple lack of other direction.

"I wanted to write but I had to make a living, and wasn't very good at driving nails," he said. "The law to this day allows people to do many things."

The law, which he calls the last of the romantic professions, "attracts and harbors dissatisfied dreamers," including one John Voelker, whose reverence for law has often shown up in his books. The law, he says, is "the busy fireman that puts out society's brush fires; that gives people a nonphysical way to discharge their hostile feelings and settle their violent differences; that spells the difference between a hostile barroom brawl and a debate; that substitutes order and predictable ritual for the rule of tooth and claw."

11

Rambling on in that precise way he has of speaking as though addressing a jury, he said the very slowness of the law, "its massive impersonality, its neutrality, its calm insistence upon proceeding according to settled procedures and ancient rules, its tendency to adjust and compromise, act to bank and cool the fires of violence and passion and replace them with order and reason."

After two years at Northern Normal in Marquette, young John Voelker enrolled as a law student at the University of Michigan. In rented tux for the traditional Crease Dance, he danced with lovely Grace Taylor from Oak Park, Illinois, slender and tall in a swishing black dress with neckline frills accentuating her face.

"I stared at her and knew the jig was up for me," John said.

Despite an invading horde of rival engineering students as they danced, and a fistfight that resulted, complete with a tumble down a staircase, ripped tuxedo, and command appearance at the dean's office, John's jig was up indeed. After his graduation in 1928 and admittance to the State Bar of Michigan, John returned to Marquette County where he served as assistant county prosecutor for two years. However, he could not forget the lovely young woman from Oak Park. He moved to Chicago, entered private practice, and married her.

The Upper Peninsula and fishing were never far from the young attorney's mind, however. In 1933, he surrendered, moved his family to Ishpeming, and ran for Marquette County prosecuting attorney. He was elected and served in that position for fourteen of the eighteen years between 1934 and 1952. "You see, there was one time when I stubbed my toe."

Between the courtroom and a growing family with the birth of three daughters, he found time to write under the name of Robert Traver, "my mother's maiden name. I thought taxpayers might think it improper for the D.A. to write under his own name on their time. I shouldn't have bothered. I could have stacked all my readers in a broom closet." But while Voelker's first three books were not exactly blockbusters, his fourth one certainly was. In 1952, the year after his return to private law practice, he successfully defended an army lieutenant charged with murdering the owner of the Lumberjack Tavern in the Marquette County village of Big Bay, who allegedly had beaten and raped the lieutenant's wife. Voelker's involvement in that case gave him the idea for *Anatomy of a Murder*, his first novel. He had little reason to believe *Anatomy* would be a hit. "My first books were out of print at the time," he recalls. During what must have been an exciting weekend in 1956, Voelker got word that his novel had been chosen for publication and that he had been named by Governor G. Mennen Williams to the Michigan Supreme Court.

As he became involved in the affairs of the high court (Justice Voelker wrote more than a hundred decisions during the three years he served), *Anatomy of a Murder* was selected for the Book-of-the-Month Club, became a best-seller (and remained so for more than a year), and was chosen to become a movie, to be shot on location in Marquette County and directed by Otto Preminger. Spending time with Jimmy Stewart, Ben Gazarra, Eve Arden, and other Hollywood stars crowded Voelker's fishing schedule, so he compromised by taking some of them fishing!

At last there was a choice of careers, with no contest! Five weeks before he was to begin a new term on the supreme court bench, Voelker resigned.

"When the baying hounds of success seemed determined to overtake and destroy me, I suddenly quit the best job I'd ever held and fled home to my native Upper Peninsula to rest and fish and brood over the books I longed to write. In my letter of resignation, I wrote Governor Williams that while other men can write my legal opinions, they can scarcely write my books."

Already to his credit were his "doorstop" books: *Troubleshooter*, *Danny and the Boys*, and *Small Town D.A.* Since *Anatomy*, he has written *Trout Madness*, *Hornstein's Boy*, *Anatomy of a Fisherman*, *Laughing Whitefish*, *The Jealous Mistress*, *Trout Magic*, *People Versus Kirk*, and many magazine and newspaper articles. Voelker, who does all his writing in longhand, on a yellow legal pad in green ink, says there are half a dozen books just waiting to be written, but fishing keeps getting in his way.

Throughout all the years, Ted Bogdan says Voelker has never lost his "little boy" side. "He sets little goals for himself, which he writes down in his notebook." Whether he's fishing, prowling the woods and back roads in search of mushrooms, or beating Bogdan at cribbage, Voelker experiences few dull moments. He sets forth in a four-wheel-drive station wagon that looks like a rolling rummage sale. Cargo on any given day might include extra hats, gloves, rain gear, a stalk of milkweed, buckets, book of county maps, plastic bags, booze, enamel cup, briefcase containing the obligatory cribbage board, camp stool with cushion, clippers, rubber boots, extra fly rods and an assortment of flies, a grill, and other assorted props for a John Voelker day.

Passionate dislikes that evoke spontaneous dissertations as he drives the back roads include more than two persons on a stretch of trout stream, traffic lights (which he'll drive for miles to avoid), the din of the city, banquets, travel in general and flying in particular. He knows that for some, travel means exciting destinations. However, in his Upper Peninsula, he is "already there." Living in the north woods is an intimate experience, one that to Voelker is not casually shared or forgotten or left behind for even a little while. Only once has he been tempted into a plane.

"I was going fishing. You see, it was a crisis to get there." It was one of those fly-in pontoon planes so popular in Ontario. Waiting with his cronies for the pilot, Voelker romantically envisioned a "British guy with leather helmet, long white scarf and high laced boots." Here came a guy in soiled khaki pants.

"Naturally, I was the last one in," Voelker said. The pilot asked Voelker to close the door. He reached for it, and discovered that the latch was no more than a modest length of wire. Wrapping it tight, he was only slightly white-knuckled until the pilot banked the aircraft and Voelker's generous frame was thrust against the wire. The door held, and the pilot excitedly asked if his passengers had seen the deer below.

"No, and don't do that again! I want sod," Voelker said.

The fishing was good on that trip, but Voelker declined to board the plane when the pilot returned to retrieve the party. Instead, the wary traveler hiked to the Algoma Central railroad track and flagged the next train for home. He hasn't flown since.

"I understand that they now have lovely flight attendants and serve booze on board, but I've heard these things are also available in other places," he says determinedly.

Every day, week, season is important to John Voelker. He forages through the seasons with small joys tucked in unexpected corners:

14

gathering red and gold autumn leaves or a sprig of balsam to slip inside the letter to a friend, pine chunks harvested for his winter fire, or winter berries for his mantel. His love affair with the north woods is without ebb, whether checking winter deer yards, searching for the first spring pussy willow, or marking with a grin the telltale signs of spring that portend the opening day of another trout season.

"Love of fishing and the outdoors is a mild form of psychosis," he says. "When fishing has ended, it's a trauma. You may be tired of it, but when Christmas comes, you hope Santa will bring you a new rod."

His *Anatomy of a Murder* notwithstanding, Voelker suspects that he will be best remembered for another piece of writing, an essay he calls "Testament of a Fisherman."

> I fish because I love to; because I love the environs where trout are found, which are invariably beautiful, and hate the environs where crowds of people are found, which are invariably ugly; because of all the television commercials, cocktail parties, and assorted social posturing I thus escape; because, in a world where most men seem to spend their lives doing things they hate, my fishing is at once an endless source of delight and an act of small rebellion; because trout do not lie or cheat and cannot be bought or bribed or impressed by power, but respond only to quietude and humility and endless patience; because I suspect that men are going along this way for the last time, and I for one don't want to waste the trip; because mercifully there are no telephones on trout waters; because only in the woods can I find solitude without loneliness; because bourbon out of an old tin cup always tastes better out there; because maybe one day I will catch a mermaid; and, finally, not because I regard fishing as being so terribly important but because I suspect that so many of the other concerns of men are equally unimportant—and not nearly so much fun.

John Voelker died on March 18, 1991.

16

3

THE INNKEEPER
TAKES A WIFE

MAKE THE SHARP TURN off Queen's Highway 17 at Rossport, Ontario, and drive back into the nineteenth century. Population is about 150, plus the innkeeper's new wife.

The village snuggles around McKay's harbor and the natural deep cut fronted by a string of wooded islands scattered along Schreiber Channel, gateway to Nipigon Bay. Cottages are from another time, quaint, low, aging structures, which look as though they were built in a hurry with rooms added randomly like an afterthought, except for a few dignified white homes on the upper street with big windows and pillars on the verandas.

Daily sounds include the ping and echo of hammers, clang of metal from the village garage, slam of doors, call of children at their games, occasional hum of tires on the highway above the village, and the whistle and rumble of trains.

Villagers occupy the dwellings, villagers trade at the general store, villagers attend the St. John Berchmans R.C. Church, and villagers lie buried under the stark white headstones in the churchyard.

"The village is in the process of gentrification," innkeeper Ned Basher comments.

Rossport Inn was not built for tourists. Basher changed it somewhat when he moved to the village and started remodeling and painting and serving three meals a day during the summer months. It changed more after he took a wife.

Then the village installed a fire hydrant between the inn and railroad tracks such as one could expect on big city streets, like a child playing dress-up, country folk putting on airs. When workers came with the hydrant, it was painted a rich shade of yellow, glorious in its newness. Basher absolutely refused to allow it to be installed in front of his inn.

"If we're going to have a fire hydrant, it's going to be red," he said. "Everybody knows fireplugs are red."

They painted it red!

Rossport Inn is a charming old hotel decked out in yellow and deep brown colors with a rusty-red roof, doorway and window boxes. Beside the inn gurgles a small stream that tumbles down the hill, running free throughout the year on its way to the harbor and Lake Superior from Little Partridge Lake in the hills above the village. A path leads from the back door of the hotel to a small waterfall and a new cedar-log sauna with picture window.

"I asked the carpenter if he could restore the old one. He said it would make a good fire for the new sauna," Basher said.

Beyond the entrance of the inn is a small lobby with a littered desk and its back wall lined with baseball caps from around the world. Basher varies his stories of the old-fashioned portraits leading to the dining room, depending on his mood. They are either his ancestors, or Sheila's, or village founders, or whoever strikes his fancy when he is bored with the same old story. However, his stories about meeting and "talking up" Sheila seldom vary.

Wooden dining room floors glisten with polish and wax. White curtains filter the sunlight streaming through the windows. Tables sport bright linen. Works by local artists adorn the walls.

Upstairs are six rooms and a shared bath for overnight guests. Floors tilt slightly toward the lake, squeaking under step. (The entire building shakes and trembles when the trains roar past.) Rooms follow an early-1920s motif, comfortable and sparkly clean with Hudson's Bay Company blankets and their telling black and red bands folded at the foot of the beds spread with colorful afghans. On the floors are brightly braided Finnish rugs.

The main upstairs attraction is the outdoor wooden porch overlooking the lake. Here one can watch villagers going about their daily tasks, search the waters for a yacht or other pleasure boats, and listen for the clatter of the next train rattling down the tracks.

One can get lost on the upstairs porch, lost in time, lost in thought, lost in reverie, with a morning sun drifting into noonday, drifting into evening with the blaze of sun sinking behind the islands before a bright moon dances into view.

Ned Basher discovered the village and inn while on a sailing trip along the north shore of Lake Superior. Sturdy build leaning to the wheel, rakish cap perched at an angle, wide smile across his handsome face, the man with the delightfully Dickensian name felt an immediate identity with the village, the same closeness he had felt with Superior when he came to Duluth as a pilot with the Minnesota Air National Guard.

"I'd been along this shore flying around in the 101 fighter-interceptors. But it's different being in a boat when you can be right down at the water where you can touch it. Flying over Rossport, I wondered who lived here. Lo and behold, fifteen years later, I'm here."

Living in Duluth on a sandbar known as Park Point, he bought a sailboat, a book of instructions, and sailed page-by-page to Bayfield, Wisconsin, by way of Port Wing and Cornucopia. The next long trip was to Sault Ste. Marie by way of Thunder Bay and Rossport. He walked up the road, pushed open the door to the inn, and enjoyed a tasty dinner.

Back home, he kept thinking of the secluded little harbor with

19

its scattering of islands. "Roaming the islands, if you see another footprint, you feel like Robinson Crusoe. On my next trip to the north shore with my brother, we saw nothing, nobody, never another boat."

Coming into the bay, the sailboat slipped between the islands and across the yacht Gunila resting 240 feet below. The palatial yacht was owned by William L. Harkness, one of the original backers of John D. Rockefeller in Standard Oil. Harkness and his guests were touring Superior in August, 1911, when the Gunila was grounded and sank off McGarvey Shoal five miles east of Rossport.

Waiting at the inn for the eastbound train to New York, innkeeper Oscar Anderson expressed his regret at the loss of the Gunila.

"Don't worry," said Harkness. "They are still building yachts."

Basher wondered if he could have taken the sinking as casually. He rounded the islands. Ahead was the village and the inn. Mooring his sailboat at the public wharf, he and his brother walked up the winding road and across the tracks, talking about the fine dinner they would share at the inn.

They found the door locked, with a "For Sale" sign in the window.

Basher complained about it so long that his brother finally suggested that he buy it himself.

"I bought it in the spring of 1983 for a song, and then I invested a couple of more songs, maybe even a complete Broadway musical, by way of renovation and repairs."

Working well into the night and starting again with the dawn, remodeling, cleaning rooms, cooking three meals a day seven days a week, he found little time for pleasures. He hired a local person to help, then discovered that his helper kept her own time clock and showed up when it was convenient. He bemoaned the way work interfered with sailing and other pleasures, and found a kindred spirit in the Norwegian bachelor, Olaf Sundland, who was working equally hard to make a success of his Forget-Me-Not gift shop.

Then one summer, romance found Olaf. A lovely tourist from Seattle stopped at the shop, and Olaf fell in love. After Olaf was married, his wife Judi added fine touches to the shop, with a tearoom in the corner where she serves hot tea and scones on blue tables with red cloths and Scandinavian paintings on the top. Suddenly Olaf was finding time to canoe and fish, and Basher was tied to the inn day and night. The innkeeper was lonely.

He waited, but no tourist brought romance to his door. Leaves faded and fell, and the inn closed for the season. Ned Basher bought an airline ticket to the Bahamas. Toward the end of his vacation, he saw dark-haired Sheila walking down the beach in a bikini.

"I looked at her and knew she could bake bread," he says with a grin.

Still, he spoke to her companion whom he had met earlier at the resort, and walked on. Departures were delayed at the airport, and Sheila came through the door.

"This time I talked her up," he says.

Sheila was on holiday with friends, and was making her way back home to Winnipeg after living seven years in London, England.

Delighted that she, too, was from Canada, Basher assured her that they were practically neighbors.

"Anything within a thousand miles can be counted as neighbors in the north country," he insists.

He told her about the village and the inn, and how he spent his summer days. Planes were called, and they headed off in different directions. Rushing back, Basher handed Sheila his business card.

"Stop in," he said, and dashed for his plane.

Spring came, and he was back in Rossport. Seeing Olaf and Judi together made him lonely; he kept remembering Sheila on the beach. Finally Basher called a friend in Winnipeg.

"I told him to find this girl named Sheila. He thought I had lost my mind."

Still, he waited.

Well into the summer, the telephone rang. A couple reserved a room. They were leaving Thunder Bay, and would be arriving late. Basher stayed up for them, eating steak and drinking beer at the long wooden table in the dining room.

"In walked this couple with a note from Sheila," he says, still somewhat astounded.

Her parents were driving to Toronto by way of Highway 17. Sheila had rummaged in her wallet for the business card, which she insists she doesn't know why she kept. She had scribbled a note to the charming, somewhat eccentric man she had met so briefly the previous winter, and asked her parents to deliver it.

With Sheila's address at last, Basher wired flowers and a one-way train ticket to Rossport.

Sheila called.

"Will you meet the train?"

"Toss your luggage out the window and it will probably land on my front steps. I'm never much more than five feet away from the tracks."

Over the next few months, Basher wooed her with such delicacies as Trout Hemingway, the inn specialty of fresh trout rolled in flour and lemon juice, covered with sesame seeds, sauted in butter and baked with basil and paprika. He did a lot of "chatting up," and learned that Sheila indeed could bake bread!

Before autumn leaves fell, innkeeper Ned Basher married his lovely Sheila in the dining room of the old hotel. He came to her dramatically clad in a handsome pair of kilts. It was the least he could do for a girl who wears a bikini so well and can also bake bread.

4

JUSTINE

THE LEGEND OF JUSTINE grows as tall as the tallest pine along Minnesota's North Shore, so I did not expect Justine to be so short. She climbed down from the pickup truck, waved to her friends and started toward her cabin door. I watched from inside.

Justine Kerfoot. Short of stature. Almost square in build now that the years have beaten a path to her door. Her face is creased by wind and exposure to all kinds of weather, but that is a price Justine gladly pays for all the years spent in the outdoors. Her hair is bobbed short around her face, not lumberjack or mannish, but stylish in the mode of the 1920s when Justine left her society balls south of Chicago and moved to the deep woods of lake country. The style fit her purpose as she learned to prowl the woods and canoe the rivers, so she never bothered to change.

When I had called her one late April day, she had invited me to stop in.

"I'll be off with friends for the afternoon. The door is always

23

open. Go inside and make yourself at home." She spoke in a low steady voice that could belong to anyone – male or female, young or old.

Justine is queen in this country where the string of lakes are its roads, and terrain denotes landmarks. There is no need for streetlights. There are no streets, and the moon and stars are all that's needed to light up the night.

Justine symbolizes Gunflint country. Justine is fast rivers pushed by rapids on their way through Minnesota's boundary waters to Lake Superior. She intimately knows the high hills and low swamps. Justine is campfires in the night with the aurora borealis dancing across the northern sky, plaintive cry of loons calling to the dawn, deep woods with moss carpeting the floors and an overhead canopy of green. Adventurer. Guide. Teacher.

"There is nothing that quite levels a person down faster than taking someone on a canoe trip. All the veneer comes right off," she says.

Justine has been removing veneer since she came up the Gunflint Trail in 1927 to a rustic fishing lodge forty-four miles north of Grand Marais, Minnesota. First she shed her own veneer, then helped free others from their shells.

On that April day, she walked lightly across the low porch and through her door. In corduroy pants with a red and black plaid mackinaw buttoned over a gray sweatshirt, she reflected the casual atmosphere of the outdoors. She smelled of fresh air and spring growth in the forest, arbutus, perhaps, or fresh boughs of lime-green tamarack.

All around the room was more of Justine: bright red Indian rugs hanging from the walls and scattered on the floor, a heavy padded willow chair, photographs, the corner near the big windows set aside for a tidy office.

Down the slope, Gunflint Lodge faces the long stretch of Gunflint Lake, which connects to the northwest with other lakes, forming Minnesota's legendary Boundary Waters. A mile and a half across the lake is Ontario where the Indians once lived. Only one is left. Not so long ago the Chippewa asked Justine where had all the others gone, knowing there was no answer, knowing they had gone the way of the times, times

when his people did everything in their own way and in their own time, an era when Indians moved back and forth across the international border as they had always done, because they had lived there before a border existed.

When Justine first arrived in the lake country, the Indians became her teachers, her friends. "I didn't know one end of a canoe from the other," she said.

The short lady of the north woods was a petite college coed, daughter of an attorney enjoying life on a small lake thirty miles from Chicago before the family lost both their Illinois homes in the stock market crash. Her life had been filled with parties, dating, golf and tennis, with hardly a worry in the world. Suddenly it was all gone.

Justine and her mother headed north to negotiate the purchase of a small fishing camp up the Gunflint Trail. It was the only thing they could afford.

The trail followed the up-and-down terrain of the country, which Justine says was laid out like a dog-team musher's trail across the rocky peaks, and the only time they saw anything like mud was when beavers dammed the road. Frost holes after spring breakup grabbed car wheels with a sudden kerplunk! Rocks heaved up every spring. Dirt seeped in the recess, and the next spring, the rocks heaved higher.

At first, cars took a beating on the trail. On cold days, engines were almost impossible to start. To warm the oil, she devised an engine starter. Justine poured kerosene in a can, placed it on a shovel, and lit it. She slid the fire under the oil pan, and let it do its job. "I had to warm the oil or I would run down the battery trying to start the car, then I'd be in a pickle."

During the early years, mother and daughter operated the fishing camp from early spring through fall while Justine's father tried to keep his law practice going back home. She says it took her about five years to adapt to her change in life-style.

"I take my hat off to Mother, a woman of that age to make that adaptation. Sure, I did, too. We came up here and there was nothing. We came from an easy environment to a definite wilderness."

She said they had to adapt in order to exist.

Justine tells of those early years and her peeling veneer in *Woman of the Boundary Waters*. She wrote the book as a result of a monthly newsletter that she sent to their summer visitors who "got to be part of the family." The book covers the time from when Chippewas lived across eight-mile-long Gunflint Lake to when only men came up the trail and finally year-round family vacationers.

Stories along the Gunflint tell about Justine paddling up rapids alone in her canoe, packing out her own thousand-pound moose, and at the lodge, building, patching, cooking – whatever needed to be done. Indians taught her the ways of the lake country: Charlie, her beloved Butchie and others.

"Butchie," she remembers with a smile. "Awbutch was her name, but the kids couldn't cut it."

"By golly, they knew how to live in the woods. I learned that their inability to write had not a heck to do with how to live up here."

She says it took a long time for the Indians to establish a trust, and if it were ever broken, trust was gone forever.

Justine and her mother started outfitting with twelve canoes. She started to guide early, as there was a financial urgency. With days spent at the paddle, heavy packs, and long portages, every part of her body ached by day's end. "I thought there must be a better way to make a living. Then suddenly everything didn't hurt any more and it became natural."

Maps were poor and inadequate. The only way she could tell their guests where to go was to map it out herself. After the summer season, she took to the lakes and rivers, studying, mapping, often alone.

She learned by doing, developing a remarkable memory of portages and rapids and falls. But put her on city streets and all she could see was fast cars. Trappers and Indians showed her cabins and where the rapids turned treacherous.

"Then I instructed our people according to their ability, with a few challenges thrown in," she said.

Since then, she has spent a lifetime teaching others to enjoy the woods without abusing it, to adapt to the woods and the environment.

"It isn't in my thinking that it's entirely the people's fault who are abusing it. Legislation is not in balance with nature."

In 1932, Justine married Bill Kerfoot who worked alongside her at the lodge. With hardly a pause in her guiding, they lost an infant son, then gave birth to Bruce, Pat and Sharon. Her Indian friends were there to help, as they had been since that first year.

Especially Butchie. "Don't let Bruce go to the minnow pond alone in June," Butchie said. "That's when bears mate and get ugly." So for the month of June, Justine always tagged along.

Kids grow well in the north country. Justine said they were "pert near" never sick, as long as they stayed north along the Gunflint. "But their first year in school, the kids got everything. With no immunity, sickness wiped off the first year."

She recalled an incident when Bruce was almost grown and was guiding parties along the river. When he failed to show up at the appointed time, their friend Charlie nonchalantly asked, "Is Bruce back yet?" He thought he would paddle over in that direction, he said. Charlie found Bruce in quick order, paddling his way home.

"My Indian friends like to save face. They never tell you they are concerned for you, but we looked after each other," Justine says.

Guests were offered guided or self-guided hikes, canoe trips, fishing trips, pontoon boat rides, lasting from one day to as long as participants desire. Justine, and now Bruce and the lodge crew, throw in a history of the area so that guests can "enjoy the woods properly." When people enjoyed the outdoors, she said they joined a special breed of people.

She talked of heavy canoes and cumbersome tents made heavier with rain. Women's outdoor clothing was unavailable then. She tried women's wool pants, and tore them to shreds on her first trip into the bush, pins holding them together as she made for the lodge. Perhaps outdoor-clothing manufacturers thought women were going to "tiptoe down the path."

She needed wool clothing, and it had to be comfortable, "so I wore men's mackinaw trousers." They were much too long for the short north woods guide. Fearing she would trip on a windfall, she took an ax, laid the pants on a stump, and gave them a whack. A hem added to the bulk, which she did not need, so the raw edges suited her fine.

In men's clothing, short-bobbed hair, ability and strength on the trail as she hoisted seventy-to hundred-pound canoes, and vocabulary that is said to sometimes match that of her clients, Justine was often mistaken for a male. She didn't bother to explain.

In 1953, Justine woke to smoke. The lodge was in flames. By

morning, it was gone. They rebuilt beside the lake, adding more canoes, more guides.

Slowly the lodge trade grew, and the season extended into winter. Justine learned to invent things, to make them work. She says even now, it causes a terrible wrenching to throw away even a "junky piece of machinery."

"I forget I can buy a new part," she said.

Chuckling, she tells of tearing apart two-cycle motors to repair and put back together again. "It came not easy. We knew we either could make do or we'd go under."

Each season welcomed lodge visitors with its own appeal. April is beautiful, she says. May is fishing season with rain and snow and bleh! June is black flies.

"They eat on me and then the tourists come and the flies eat on them because they are tired of me by then."

Winter brings skiers and snowmobilers. For Justine, snowmobiles will never replace a dog team where she could "mosey along and enjoy things," compared to a fast ride down the trail without seeing anything. Although she once regularly went ice fishing with the Indians, she equates it to a way to get "damn good and cold." But the lodge is there for all.

"So that's kind of the way it developed in the woods," she said, leaning back for a moment, slight smile playing at the corner of her mouth. "Except that I still go out and try to break ice before it is thawed."

Her children feel better if someone goes along, but if there is nobody up to adventure, Justine goes anyway.

She feels comfortable with me, and a gleam warms her eyes as she confidently says, "Do you know where I was today? I knew a trail that led to a lake that my friends didn't know about. They had a truck they didn't mind getting dirty, with a canoe thrown in the back.

"They hadn't thought of canoeing today, so didn't put in the paddles. But I knew I would with or without paddles."

She stopped for a moment, watching sun fading through the windows. Then she went on. She had found two sticks for paddles. They pushed off to explore, three elderly people miles from nowhere, three people young at heart on a Sunday lark, three people with no veneer.

The stick oars worked well as they skimmed across the water in the bay. Rounding a peninsula, they poked along the shoreline, watched the arrival of the first ducks of spring, watched a dipping sun. Reluctantly, they finally turned back.

Ice had formed on the bay, with a good fifty feet between the canoeists and shore. Justine mischievously told how they alternately broke ice with the stick and paddled, finally making shore.

"So we introduce another spring. . . ."

I recall her words to friends as they drove away.

"What are you doing next Sunday?" she had called. "Let's try it again."

5

THE CRYING CABIN, PART 1

THE GREAT-GRANDSON of a mighty Indian chief may have been considered a good catch for some men's daughters before the turn of the century, but Horatio Seymour had his mind set on royalty of another strain.

Seymour fretted about rearing his family in the wild untamed north woods of Michigan's Upper Peninsula when his uncle, the governor of New York, asked him to go west to manage family interest in the Michigan Land and Iron Company. Seymour and his proud wife were accustomed to a more genteel way of life than that offered by the brawling lumber and mining town they found at Marquette in 1882. Not even the elite of Ridge Street measured up to the expectations of the couple who counted presidents and near-presidents among their ancestors.

The small, dark man of fragile health built a house in the best part of the city overlooking the bay of Lake Superior. Beyond the spacious gardens, behind the fretted scrolls and hedged window, the proud and queenly Abigail Adams Seymour, descendant of John Adams and Abigail Smith, shunned all social functions among the "base pioneers" of Marquette. She refused to bow to northern fashions or allow Mary and Horatio, Jr., to play with children in the town. She sent them back East for their education.

When dark-eyed Mary returned from Eastern schools with her younger brother, the Seymours feared that her bubbling, friendly spirit might attract some of the local youths into thoughts of romance and matrimony. To protect them from influence of local society and youth, Seymour built a cabin at the base of Sugarloaf Mountain along the shore of Lake Superior several miles west of Marquette. The summer Mary was seventeen and "Rakey" fifteen, the ailing Seymour took them over the old lumber road to the summer cabin at the cove.

Mary lifted her heavily starched Eastern skirts and skipped along the moss-cushioned path toward the cabin. The strong, low-roofed cabin of hewn logs nestled in a dark stand of virgin spruce and hemlock, with wide porch opening toward a jutting point of granite, which formed a natural cove and protected it from the inland sea. The girl nodded to a tall, handsome bearded man with fierce, steady gaze hired as their guardian and caretaker.

He was Henry St. Arnauld, known as Santinaw, pioneer land-looker and outstanding woodsman of the north. Santinaw was descended from Mamongeseda, who had led a party of Indian warriors for two thousand miles from La Pointe, Wisconsin, to Quebec, where they fought in the ranks of Montcalm on the Plains of Abraham. His great-grandfather was Waubojeeg, chief of the Ojibway's Reindeer Clan, and his father was the French-Canadian fur trader Edward St. Arnauld who had married Marie Des Carreaux, granddaughter of Waubojeeg.

More Indian by nature than guaranteed by his one-quarter Indian blood, Santinaw approached in height his towering ancestors. At fifty-two, he was straight as an arrow, swarthy, strong beyond the strength of normal men. He was swift of foot, a woodsman who knew intimately every growing thing and every fish that swam the streams.

For years, he had roamed the forests for weeks on end, living off the land. But once he came back to town, he headed straight

for a barber for a careful trimming of his long, flowing beard and straight dark hair, which fell across his shoulders. Only then did he hurry up the hill to his two-story home on the edge of town where wife and family were waiting. Then death struck. Twice. He buried a daughter, and four years later his wife.

Santinaw lingered in Marquette through the summer of 1898. Even though his other two daughters were almost grown, he was reluctant to leave them so soon after the newest grave was dug under the pines. Nor was he ready for the forest. When Seymour offered him the guardian job at Cove Cottage, a despondent

Santinaw accepted. He found some measure of contentment with the lake lapping at the sand stretch of beach down the path or pounding out its fury against the boulders, with wind whispering in the trees and the mountain to flex his muscles upon.

The Seymour youngsters were avid pupils of nature. For three summers, Santinaw returned to the cottage to tutor Mary and Rakey on the lore of the woods, of plants, herbs and trees. Long hours slipped away as they hiked the animal trails and scaled the highest boulders and hills along the lake.

Seymour's health continued to fail, and he was soon confined to a wheelchair. Occasionally he ventured his chair along a packed rut of the logging road that approached the cabin, or pushed up the trail leading to Sugarloaf as far as the incline allowed.

"Would you like to see the top?" asked Santinaw as he watched him gazing upward.

The little man considered the rugged mountain strewn with jagged boulders, and shrugged. But Santinaw found a way. For days he hacked through underbrush and trees, clearing a path that skirted boulders and spanned rock cuts. On Seymour's next trip to the cove, Santinaw tied him to the wheelchair and pushed him all the way to the top.

Meanwhile, Mary had blossomed into a young woman. With the only man in her life the lonely Santinaw, Mary fell in love in the summer of her twentieth year. "I pressed myself on Henry," she said in later years.

He shook his head in disbelief. He protested the difference in their ages; the still handsome Santinaw was fifty-five.

"My ways are Indian ways," he said.

"Then your ways will be my ways," she insisted.

Finally in October as the forest glowed rainbows of crimson, orange and gold, she persuaded him to run away. Henry said they should catch the train for Houghton eighty miles west where they could register for a marriage license.

Mary scribbled a hasty note to her parents and left it pinned to a sewing cushion. Her father found it and stopped the train. Word of his daughter's choice of husbands had already reached

34

Marquette. Disgrace! The entire town held their sides and laughed behind their hands. Too good for their sons? Royalty, indeed!

Mrs. Seymour fought against the marriage to the end. But there was no forgiveness from Mary's stern father.

Santinaw took his bride to his house in town. A comfortable home, two-story, yet beyond the social circles. His daughters tried to teach their youthful stepmother to cook and perform other household chores. Mary tried, neighbors recalled. Even after the birth of their baby girl, she tried not to complain when Henry's work took him to the woods for weeks on end.

At least Rakey and the rest of Marquette's youth profited from the marriage. The socially inclined and even the Seymours said if rigid rules could produce this marriage, it was time to reevaluate. There was an immediate clatter of lowering social barriers.

Two years later, Mary heard that her father was very ill. The family was returning East. Mary stayed.

In 1905, the Seymours knocked at her door with word that her father was dying in New York. He was begging for Mary. She must come at once.

Henry was in the woods. What should she do? She could not leave a personal note. Henry couldn't read. Finally she packed baby Marie's clothing and without a note or farewell for Henry, headed for her father's bedside. When Santinaw returned, his wife and child were gone.

Seymour lingered on for eighteen months before he died. By then, Mary's resolve had weakened. Her family pleaded for her to wait a while longer to return; Marquette was no place to raise a little girl. A while longer. And longer.

Mary enrolled in McGill University, and later Syracuse, studying the Indian language and poring over plant lore she had first learned from Santinaw. Perhaps she could share these things with Henry when she returned.

Later her mother died, leaving a large inheritance to Mary and granddaughter Marie, who was becoming a young lady. Santinaw's daughter rejected her Indian blood and heritage, forbidding her mother to speak of her father or the past.

35

"I didn't want to grieve her, so I refrained," Mary later said.

Marie made the matrimonial match her mother had missed, becoming the wife of a prominent New York attorney.

Mary pursued her studies while working at the Smithsonian Institution in Washington, then headed west. For five years she wandered across Wyoming's deserts and mountains, collecting plant specimens and studying Indian lore. Years drifted past. She often thought of her husband along Lake Superior's shores. She wished he could read.

Twenty-five years after she had left his house in Marquette, she tore open a letter from Henry's niece, Mrs. Peter Clyne, of L'Anse. Mary's eighty-four-year-old husband was dying.

When the family told Santinaw that Mary was coming, the old man's shoulders sagged.

"Why, after all these years?" he asked.

A portly matron descended the steps of the train and hailed the village's only taxi for the short trip to her husband's side.

She knelt beside him. "I have always loved you, Henry," she said to the white-haired old man. Finally, Henry reached to clutch her hand.

The Clyne household was already overflowing with relatives. Mary found a room with cousins two doors down. She visited her husband daily, often scolding him for not exercising better care of himself, and especially for his grooming habits.

Each morning Santinaw splashed his head and beard with water until they were dripping wet, then walked outside in the freezing cold to empty the wash basin. He would step back through the door with hair and long flowing beard frozen stiff.

"You'll catch your death," she said.

Santinaw persisted. He had not been able to stop his wife from heading East those many years before, but he stubbornly continued his grooming ritual his way.

Santinaw was handsome and straight as an arrow until the end. And he took his own time dying. He regained some measure of health and lived for almost three years after Mary's return.

After Santinaw's death, Mary lingered in the area that she had deserted so many years before. She rented an apartment in

Marquette, bought a sailboat, and sailed down to the cove where she had fallen in love.

In 1934, Mary Seymour St. Arnauld walked past the gingerbread house overlooking the bay where her parents had lived, then stopped at the smaller house where Santinaw had taken her as a bride. She wondered if anyone had ever understood her, if she had understood herself, or why she had stayed away so long.

There was nobody left to understand, except perhaps young John Tobin, the new caretaker at Cove Cottage. He loved the cottage, the cove, the lake, and rugged Sugarloaf Mountain at its back. He had listened patiently to her stories of Cove Cottage, of her Henry and her return. Perhaps he would understand.

She found him at the log cabin under the towering hemlocks. She was leaving, she told him. Back East again. Farewell. She reached into her ample pocket for a favorite book of poems by Lew Saratt. Tobin held the slender volume in his hands as she walked away. It fell open to the marked pages Mary knew so well: "God, let me flower as I will. . . .

6

THE CRYING CABIN, PART 2

SOME FOLKS SAID THE strange crying was caused by the wind fresh off Lake Superior squeezing through the cove where the Indian once moored the rich man's boats. Some said the sound came from behind the spot where the cabin once stood. But the ones who have heard the crying in the night shake their heads and tremble.

Only bare traces of the spot (called Crying Cabin in recent years) stand in the tall thimbleberry bushes beneath the dark spruce and hemlock trees west of Marquette.

Footsteps along the narrow path are cushioned by ages of peat and undergrowth. Roots twist into hidden traps, reaching up to snag the unsuspecting hiker who ventures through the woods on the far side of Sugarloaf Mountain.

Most of the logs tumbled from the cabin walls years ago, felled by roaring blasts of wind howling down the cove, or perhaps shoved aside by the eerie forces some folks say scared the undertaker and the priest away, and took the life of the young student.

Someone added cheap boards and tar paper to the skeletal frame left standing over the stone fireplace that the Indian built.

But all is ashes now, scattered to the winds on a winter's night when the roof collapsed under a weight of snow, and the flames in the fireplace licked the weathered timbers into a roaring fury.

If the seven students on a winter campout had heard the legends of the Crying Cabin, they paid no heed. No one spoke of noises that night, but one will never again hear the strange crying in the wind. He died underneath the snow.

John Tobin of Marquette knows many of the legends. He was caretaker in the early 1920s when legends of the Indian and the rich man's lovely daughter were still new. He later met the rich man's daughter when she returned to the side of her dying husband. He said at first, there seemed to be nothing mysterious about the log cabin underneath the drooping hemlocks, except for the stories of the romance and the lonesome Indian.

One winter, Tobin's friend Tom Kelly took sick and dropped out of school. Kelly's father worried about the dark depressions that hounded the young man. He asked Tobin to see after him for the winter, and the two moved into the cabin.

Snows and freezing wind lashed across Lake Superior and beat upon the cabin door. They piled another log on the fire, and slept cozy warm.

Tobin recalled Kelly's phobia about fire. He fussed unnecessarily about the burning logs, always making sure the sparks were brushed back from the hearth's edge.

Friends joined them at the cabin. Once, as they walked along a wet trail, someone dropped a burned-out match. Kelly turned back suddenly and angrily ground the fireless match into the mud with his heel.

The dark overhanging branches of the twisted hemlocks seemed a natural place for ghost stories, and the friends spent hours trying to frighten one another out of their wits. They moved from stories to Ouija boards and extrasensory perception.

One starless night, Tobin and his four friends decided to experiment with extrasensory perception. They chose Kelly to be "it."

40

As he waited outside the cabin for them to instigate the plan, the three pondered over the least likely thing Kelly might be forced to do. They remembered his phobia of fire.

Someone suggested having him move the lantern from the center of the table. Kelly always made certain it was set squarely in the middle. He refused to remain in the cabin if it was anywhere near the edge.

Someone said, "When Kelly comes back into the room, have him move the lantern to the extreme southeast rim of the table." They chuckled in boyish delight, and called Kelly. Kelly opened the door. They concentrated. Kelly walked straight for the table without a moment's hesitation, and moved the lantern to the edge of the southeast corner. Tobin said he and his friends stopped the game.

Before the winter was over, the friends delved once more into the mystic. While Kelly tended the fire, they pledged that, after death, they would each try to find their way back to Cove Cottage. Each promised that if he were the surviving member of the clan, he would return to receive the messages from the world beyond.

Then they disbanded, each going his own way.

Tobin said he heard no ghostly figures moving in the dark, but there prevailed a strange, uneasy something that seemed to move through the fog that gathered on the point and through the trees. If anyone heard a woman weeping, nobody talked about it.

Tobin left the cabin to work on the ore boats of Lake Superior.

Kelly died.

The rest all but forgot their pledges made around Kelly's fire.

The wind howled around the cabin. It tore at the wooden steps and the screen on the door. Logs rotted. Winter snow and summer sun crept through the holes in the porch roof. New owners bought the property, and occasionally picnicked at the cove.

One day, a tall young man came hiking over the western rim of the mountain. He spotted the cabin crumbling under the hemlocks and shook his head at the decay.

He located the owner in Chicago. She refused to sell, but offered to let him use the cabin if he wanted to fix it up.

Stewart is not his real name; even now, he refuses to have his name linked with the cabin. Stewart hauled in boards and nails to make the cabin waterproof. On afternoon trips to the cove, the cabin seemed to welcome Stewart and his wife.

They found the remnants of the red icehouse the Indian had tended at the turn of the century. The pinion for tying up the boat was still secured in the boulders at the cove.

Then Stewart decided to spend the night. He banked the fire and watched the flickering flames as the sun ducked early behind the tall forest.

The curtain of night fell black. Then he heard the crying, and icy chills crept along his spine. It sounded like a woman sobbing in the night.

He dashed to the door and threw it open wide. Flashing a beam of light into the darkness, he searched the yard, the icehouse, the trees.

Nothing. The crying always seem to be one flicker beyond his beam of light.

The sobbing stopped sometime in the night.

On other nights at the cabin, Stewart said he heard mumbling voices. They came intermittently with the crying. Sometimes they were silent for nights on end. Sometimes there were bloodcurdling screams.

On one visit to the cove, Stewart was accompanied by a friend, a Catholic priest. During the visit, one of the priest's parishioners died. The local undertaker found the priest at the Crying Cabin at twilight. While the priest gathered up his possessions, a scream pierced the air.

"The undertaker talks about it yet," Stewart said. "He said nothing could persuade him to stay there overnight."

Others who claim to have heard the screams said it was probably no more than a bobcat who prowled the woods, and the noises had nothing to do with the legend of the cove.

Finally, when Stewart's wife refused to go there again, he decided to solve the mystery once and for all. He loaded a backpack with a week's supplies and hiked over the mountain trail.

At the cabin, he probed the eaves for possible holes where the wind might squeeze through its eerie sounds. He searched along the cove for cracks and crevices in the boulders that could produce the crying in the night. He looked to the waters of Lake Superior for the source of voices, and up the chimney for the mysterious sobbing screams.

Stewart searched for five days and found nothing. He noted everything in his diary, describing in detail his methodical daily searches.

Then, on the fifth night, he sat by lamplight watching the flames licking up the chimney. The sound of muffled footsteps came softly through the log walls, then with a solid tread seemed to walk across the back porch.

Stewart leaped for the door and yanked it open. The porch, the night, was empty.

Then he heard the voices in the cove. He ran around the cabin; the voices were always one step ahead. Sudden fear squeezed his breath away as he remembered the cabin door left ajar. He turned and ran back inside.

The cabin was empty. He quickly bolted the door. The voices finally faded into the night, and he again heard the crying woman. She cried until the dawn.

Stewart picked up his pen. With trembling fingers, he scribbled the last notes in his diary and tucked it into the bottom of his pack.

In the light of morning, he hiked rapidly over the hills with the pack fastened to his back.

At home, he reached for the diary to note his time of arrival. He searched through the entire pack. He spilled the contents onto the floor. The diary was gone.

Stewart hiked back over the hills. He checked the trail and searched the cabin, finding no sign of the notebook. "I left the cabin and never went back," he said.

Shingles rotted once again. More logs caved in. All traces of the red icehouse disappeared.

Someone nailed up a stray board here and there, and used the structure as an occasional picnic shelter from the rain.

In the late 1970s, snow was banked eight feet deep around the cabin when the students hiked in from across the hills. They stacked logs in the old fireplace and waited for the flames to dance along the hearth. They grew warm and tired, and threw their sleeping bags on the floor beside the fire.

Outside,the temperature rose to above freezing. The snow changed to light rain, adding more weight to the heavy snow deposited on the creaking roof.

Three of the campers watched the sagging of the timbers, and moved to their own tents outside. During the night, another student worried about the sagging roof and joined them.

Light rain pelted the roof all night. Fog swirled along the cove and mingled with the smoke and glowing embers of the fire.

The sun was making a feeble effort to climb over the mountain when the roof collapsed on the three sleeping young men. One escaped from a hole in the south side of the room. Another woke up under falling timbers and wet snow.

The third never knew.

After rescue teams fought their way through chest-deep snow, they left the cabin in the cove. Fire from the embers spread to the remaining timbers, eating away until only the fireplace remained.

Tobin heard about the fire, and remembered Kelly. He never met Stewart, nor heard his story. He thought about the vow made many years ago, and the promise to return for possible signals from the others.

They are all dead. He is the last one left who made the pact at Cove Cottage. The Indian died in 1932, followed by the rich man's daughter approximately twenty years later.

Tobin is a reasonable man, with the temperament of a poet. He is agile, able to climb hills with ease. He could walk across the mountain to the cove – if he desired.

When he talks about the pact made at the cove, he shakes his head and looks away.

"I'll never go back there," he said.

7

DROP DEAD PLEASE

OLD-TIMERS STILL have a lot of tales to tell. Such as Sonia Saari Strong, who proved her point with stories of when the Indians helped her mother to elope, of a redheaded woman who blinked, and of the corpse in the rocking chair.

The Ishpeming native with the snapping brown eyes was one of eleven children born to the town's first Finnish undertaker.

Her father, Gustavious Adolph Saari, spotted his bride, Susanna Hongisto, after she came from the old country to cook in her uncle's logging camp near Cedarville in Michigan's Upper Peninsula. The lumberjack wasn't the only one who noticed her. When Susanna stopped at the store in the town to buy supplies, the grocer tried to corner her among the vegetables.

Chippewa squaws watching from the front door dropped their usual stoic expressions, pulled out their knives, and rushed to her rescue. A special understanding developed and the women became fast friends.

When Susanna fell in love with the dashing Gustavious, she begged her uncle's permission to marry. The uncle didn't want to lose his cook and objected so strongly that the couple decided to elope. Susanna enlisted the help of her Indian friends.

On the day of the planned escape, the Indians met the couple outside the logging camp and escorted them all the way to Cedarville. They sneaked the newlyweds into a deserted log cabin in the woods where the Saaris made their first home.

The tribe camped nearby and helped the Saaris as they worked the woods, with Gustavious downing the trees and Susanna peeling logs. After the birth of their first son, they counted out their savings: six hundred dollars! Time to move on.

They heard the iron-mining town of Ishpeming was booming with opportunity. When the train pulled into the station, they heard a different story. Everyone was walking the streets, idled by a crippling strike at the mines. Saari bought a log house and invested the remainder of his savings in a furniture store.

As more babies arrived, he moved his family to a larger house overlooking the city. The versatile lumberjack also expanded his furniture store to include an undertaking parlor. He went away to school, took the state examination in Lansing, and opened his parlor in 1899.

Susanna was too busy having babies to help with the business. Saari, ever a strict disciplinarian, called in the kids. Everyone was assigned a job. Alma manned the blood pump in the funeral parlor. Sonia combed the women's hair.

"We never thought to object," Sonia said. "When Pa said do it, we did it."

A fire in 1909 threatened to destroy the Saari funeral business while he was out of town. Susanna rushed down the hill and ripped all the expensive silks from the coffins so all would not be lost.

After the town rescue department brought the fire under control, Susanna didn't dare to waste the fabric. Pondering for only a moment, she dragged out the sewing machine and fashioned dresses and shirts for all her children. They looked so splendid in their silks and finery that she called in a neighbor to take their picture. One brother was missing. Hank hid in the

outhouse where no one could find him until the film was all
snapped and the photographer had gone home.
Tragedy struck the family when the mother died while giving

birth to her eleventh child. The undertaker was so stricken that he called in a special artist from Wisconsin to prepare Susanna for burial.

After that, the children were even more committed to their chores in the parlor. One day, little Sonia was mesmerized by the long, flowing red hair of one unfortunate customer. She brushed and brushed, long after the usual brushing time. Suddenly the redheaded woman's eyes fluttered, then opened wide. Sonia looked down into the beautiful blue eyes and screamed for her father.

Saari screamed for the doctor. An hour later, the doctor pronounced her dead again. He said the brushing had apparently revived her for a short time.

Saari had his own comment. "The next one that comes in here had better be dead," he roared at the doctor.

The corpse in the rocking chair presented a different problem.

The Saari phone rang early one stormy morning.

"My mother died last night," said a woman from one of the rural mine locations. "I want her buried in Ishpeming. Can you come after her?"

Saari took a wary look at the howling blizzard outside, but promised to try. He harnessed his horse to the sleigh and threw the dead basket in the back. Fighting his way through the storm, he took several wrong turns before locating the isolated log cabin with a lean-to porch at the back.

The woman answered the pounding on the door and ushered the shivering undertaker to the stove. She warmed him up with steaming coffee as he fumbled through the necessary forms with icy fingers. Finally, he looked around the toasty room and asked where the body lay.

The woman said she had always heard that a body should be kept in a cold room. Because both cabin rooms were heated by the roaring fire to ward off the blizzard, she had moved her mother to the back porch.

Saari pulled up the collar of his great coat and opened the door. Four-foot snowdrifts covered several mounds along the porch, but he saw no sign of his potential client. "I hate to trouble you, but just where is your mother?"

Shivering in her sweater, the woman leaned through the open door and pointed to the tallest snow-covered mound in the corner.

"Under there," she said, and darted back inside.

Saari started shoveling. Underneath, he found the corpse sitting in a rocking chair, frozen stiff. He gently pried, hoping to loosen her enough to lay her in the basket. Nothing moved. He pried harder. Nothing moved, except the rockers, which suddenly creaked against the icy floor.

He pulled himself upright, and timidly knocked again. Explaining the situation, he asked permission to bring her mother back inside until he could thaw her from the chair.

"I'll not have all that ice and snow in my kitchen," said the woman as she slammed the door against the cold.

The undertaker picked up the body, rocking chair and all, and made his way through the drifts to the sleigh. The horse moved restlessly as he lifted the chair onto the back. Saari climbed aboard, jiggled the lines and headed for Ishpeming.

Down the road a way, he spied the shadowy figure of a man trudging through the swirling snow. A farmer was bravely trying to make his way to town. Ever obliging, Saari stopped and offered him a ride. As the farmer climbed up beside him, he nodded solemnly to the woman passenger.

The sleigh jogged over and through the drifts toward town, bouncing off the frozen ruts and hidden rocks. The rocker rocked back and forth. The farmer glanced nervously over his shoulder, and back to Saari. The rocker rocked on.

"Don't you have an extra blanket?" he asked. "She looks frozen."

"She is," said Saari. "She died this morning."

The farmer jerked his head straight ahead, his hands visibly trembling through his mittens as they grasped for the edge of the sleigh.

"Stop this horse," he called out hoarsely as he half rose to lift one leg toward the ground. "I'd rather walk!"

The last Saari saw of the farmer, he was thrashing through the snow toward home, occasionally glancing over his shoulder as the old lady rocked on toward Ishpeming. He also had a tale to tell.

8

MAGIE

SOMETIMES AS THE PURPLE rays of evening paint the surface of a mirrored lake in Minnesota's Boundary Waters Canoe Area with night creeping among the marshes and the pines, canoeists claim to glimpse the shadowed figure of a man and dog in the flicker of a campfire on the shore. Folks who claim to know the wilderness, who know the legends, nod and smile.

"Bill Magie and Murphy up to tricks again," says folks who know.

Of all persons who leaned to the paddle and set a canoe skimming across the Boundary Waters Canoe Area, Magie knew the wilderness best. For years, he worked out of Ely as a full-time guide, one of the best guides and conservationists who ever canoed Minnesota waters. To return to the wilderness was a promise he made before he died, a promise mixed with tall tales he spun around campfires during the seventy years he prowled the waterways and back country.

As board member and early supporter of Voyageurs National

Park Association, executive secretary of Friends of the Boundary Water Wilderness, guide of the famous and not so famous, Magie fought to preserve the wilderness. He was also a spinner of tall tales and lover of everything wild.

When President Lyndon B. Johnson signed the federal wilderness bill in 1964, he invited Magie to attend. Magie had fought eight years for the bill, but he couldn't make it. He was off on a canoe trip.

He and Murphy the spaniel shared many adventures before cancer and old age returned them to a cabin in the northern woods of Wisconsin. Magie propped his battered old canoe near the door, waiting, yearning to paddle across the lake and off into the wilderness once again.

With Murphy crouched between his master's legs, the team had paddled more than 125 canoe trips together. The spaniel occasionally took command from the bow, leaning forward, ears flopping in the wind, tongue lapping at the water as spray settled fine droplets on his heavy black and white coat.

Magie managed the portages while Murphy checked the trail ahead. The small, wiry man hefted hundred pound canoes with ease, with a fifty to hundred pound pack strapped to his back.

He first saw what is now the Boundary Waters Canoe Area in 1909 at the age of seven. His father, a surgeon, was called from Duluth to treat a lumber official who had been crushed when a logging chain broke and pinned him underneath a big red pine log.

The lumber company dispatched a special train for the first leg of the 18–hour journey, then transferred the doctor and party to a boat for the trip across Fall Lake. The man died midway back across the lake. Because Magie's father had tried so gallantly to save him, the lumber company executives extended the Magies an open invitation to return and fish.

For the next twelve years, Magie canoed the area now legislated as a wilderness area and Ontario's bordering Quetico Provincial Park, first with his father and later with high school and college friends. Trips with school friends were supervised by a teacher he called Phillips. When Phillips died in 1922, Magie took over as guide.

The elder Magies tried to add a bit of polish and formal education to their backwoods-loving son by sending him to schools out East. According to Magie, he was kicked out of some of the best.

"At finishing school, I roomed with Reggie Vanderbilt of the

New York Vanderbilts. That was always good for twenty-five or fifty dollars from Mother," Magie said.

Reggie's friendship proved even more profitable when he talked Magie into ordering a new Stutz Bearcat and sending the car bill to Magie's father.

At Princeton, Magie and Joe Mayo of the Mayo Clinic family livened up a university dance by inviting two Follies stars as their dates. Princeton was not ready for such glamour.

Back home in 1920, flying fever hit Magie. He ordered a "souped-up Jennie stick-and-wire biplane, which I learned to fly, mostly by myself." Magie said Orville Wright organized the National Aeronautical Association and the Aero Club of America. He applied for a flying license.

"A man came around to see if I could fly. I paid twenty five dollars for license number seven, signed by Orville."

A few months later, Magie delighted onlookers and angered local police by looping the Jennie through the Duluth Aerial Bridge, with an Immelmann on the top for extra thrills (half of a loop with a 180-degree twist). "I won a fifty dollar bet, but the police and mother weren't too happy about it," he said with his usual grin.

With a mining engineering degree in his pocket from the University of Virginia, Magie landed a job with U.S. Steel at Coleraine. He spent weekends tearing up and down the roads to Duluth in his Bearcat, with canoe side trips to the boundary waters.

In 1926, when the International Joint Commission was looking for someone to define the uncertain Minnesota-Ontario border, they came looking for Magie. The existing border represents his work.

He also worked the back country of the Superior National Forest around Ely and Grand Marais. For four years he worked with the U.S. Corps of Engineers investigating water rights of ports on the southern shores of Lake Superior from Sault Ste. Marie, Michigan, to Grand Portage, Minnesota.

Then he joined forces with Sigurd Olson to organize the Friends of the Wilderness, and to promote the Isaac Walton

League. "I saw what was happening to the wilderness, and didn't want to lose it," Magie said.

He played no favorites, as his son Pat can attest. When Pat landed a seaplane in a wilderness area restricted to motorized travel, Magie had him arrested.

Among the famous, it became almost a status symbol to canoe with Magie through the Boundary Waters Canoe Area: Zsa Zsa Gabor, Mary Margaret McBride, Hubert Humphrey, Margaret Mead, and many more. With a faraway look in his eye and a grin on his face, he admitted that Zsa Zsa was among his favorite campers.

He tailored each trip to the experience of the parties, roughing it, fishing along the way, "sometimes patching beat-up canoes with Band-Aids," he admitted.

At nightfall, he left camp-making to the rest while he handled the pots and pans over a glowing campfire. Menus included fish. "If I stacked all the fish I've cleaned, they would reach around the world," he said.

Camps sometimes had uninvited wildlife guests. He recalled one trip with several governors of southern states "who were hiding out from the president because of some segregation bill. We took the canoes down the Moose River to Iron, then Crooked lakes. Canoes were loaded with luggage, fishing tackle, and a heavy cardboard box they had brought along. I asked what they wanted for lunch, and they said they'd have the box. Inside, wrapped in a khaki blanket, were twelve bottles of Johnny Walker Black Label. We got to Agnes Lake that night, but it took a while because of the Black Label."

After a feast on walleye and northern pike, Magie piled the pots and pans on top of the "grub sack" before turning in. During the night, a bear with two cubs came calling. Magie said he awoke, ran from the tent, "gave the bear a kick in the fanny, and the whole family took off."

The following night, Magie made camp on an island with no sign of bears.

A few days later, he noticed the food larder was low. Potatoes were down to a handful, with one loaf of bread and three bottles of Black Label. He hiked to a friend's cabin that stood nearby to "borrow potatoes from the stock." As he returned to camp, he saw a deer munching from their food supply. Magie chuckled over the sight of the South Carolina governor chasing the deer in an attempt to retrieve their last loaf of bread.

And after evening meals as twilight painted shadows on the waters and darkness mingled with the mist, the guide spun tall tales for his guests. His favorite was the story of Broken-Neck Charlie and the moose. "When I was sixteen years old, Father and I were holed up in a logging camp at Christine Lake, hunting with Broken-Neck Charlie as our guide," he would begin. Magie told the tale again shortly before he died. He slouched in the outdoor swing of his cabin in the Wisconsin woods, hands tucked resolutely in his armpits, fishing hat tugged down over his ears, Murphy sleeping at his feet.

Magie said the hunting party was after moose, with nothing but tracks in new snow to show for their troubles. After two weeks of unsuccessful hunting, he asked permission from his father to hunt alone.

"About 10:30 that morning, I saw new tracks as big as pie plates," said Magie. "I followed half a mile into the woods where they led off into a swamp. There I stopped to have a conference with myself.

"Broken-Neck Charlie always said 'most hunters big damn fools. They walk through swamp and never see moose. Charlie walk around swamp. Moose comes out other side. Charlie shoots moose.'

"I followed Charlie's example. I walked around the swamp. Moose came out the other side. I shot once, twice. Down he went, ker-plunk."

Magie embellished the tale, with the moose up again, trailing off through the snow, down again, with the final shot on the last shell made while the hunter leaned against a white birch tree for support. He re-created the ritual of cleaning the animal, with a yard of flannel dipped into the snow to wash the cavity, pushing and tugging to hoist the legs high enough to insert the forked stick that would hold the cavity open.

"After I took time out to eat my lunch, it was three o'clock by my dollar Ingersoll watch," he went on. "It was spitting snow, and I was trying to decide if I should leave the moose and follow the trail back to camp, or head cross-country.

"I reloaded the gun and started off down the trail. When I saw how fast the snow was covering my tracks, I sat down and had another conference with myself. I decided to retrace my steps. By the time I got back to the moose, it was pitch dark.

"I built a fire and waited. My belly was warm and my fanny was cold, so I sat on a log and built two fires so both sides would keep warm.

"With snowflakes coming down the size of quarters, I figured it was time to bunk for the night. Out of desperation, I cut spruce and balsam boughs and stacked them inside the warm cavity of the moose. Then I crawled in and laid the rifle by my side."

Magie claimed that when he awoke the next morning, the carcass had frozen shut. After relating lengthy experiences best left to Magie's special telling, he said he heard gunshots several ridges over. The search party was on its way! They eventually discovered the moose, but did not spy Magie trapped inside.

"While some of the party continued the search, Broken-Neck Charlie tied the moose around the neck, hitched him to a wagon, and gave me a free ride back to camp. As they prepared to dress the moose, I heard a big whack of the cleaver. Every time they sawed and hacked, I bellered and groaned from the inside.

"Charlie yelled for Father. 'This moose ain't dead yet,' Charlie yelled.

"About that time, Father suspected something. He pried open the sides of the moose and peeked inside. By the time he dragged me out and got through with me, I was hollering aplenty," Magie said, concluding his favorite tale.

Magie tried to adapt to domesticity. He married a nurse from Duluth. His wife Lucille did most of the raising of their four daughters and son Pat.

Times changed from the days when the man and dog roamed the BWCA for weeks at a time without meeting another party. With heavier use, canoeists often waited in line at summer portages for half a day.

In the early 1970s, Magie and Murphy flew in to Powell Lake

just east of the Quetico boundary. They snowshoed to the Gunflint Trail, man and dog treading the snows together, by way of lakes Mack, Munro, Cullen, Ross, Bitchu, Saganagons and Saganaga.

Then he left the wilderness legacy to others. On August 18, 1979, friends honored his lifelong work with a plaque at Farm Lake near Ely. It reads:

> Think on this land of lakes and forests.
> It cannot survive Man's greed
> Without man's selfless dedication.
> William H. Magie
> Friend of the Wilderness
> Devoted most of his life to this cause,
> Now it is yours.

9

ONCE UPON A TRAIN

THE ALGOMA CENTRAL RAILWAY has changed little since I first climbed aboard in the mid-1970s. Big yellow diesel engines still follow the way of the bear from home base in Sault Ste. Marie, Ontario, and north through bush country to Hearst: tourist trains to spectacular Agawa Canyon, locals to the end of the line, freights lumbering in between.

And before the "All aboard," come trappers, hunters, fishermen, railroad crew, senior citizens on tour, prospectors, miners, summer campers, canoeists, and a collage of residents from towns and villages served by the ACR.

Construction of the 298-mile line began in 1899. It pushed northward through the rugged Laurentian Hills from Sault Ste. Marie following timber and mining until it reached Hearst in 1914. The train squirms its way northward through canyons and rocky gorges for almost two hundred miles until it climbs from the hills where bones of the earth poke through and onto the straightway of muskeg reaching northward to Hearst. Tall pine, hemlock, spruce and balsam scatter through the hardwood to mellow the forest in refreshing green before blazing forth in autumn color, then spread nude branches for winter garlands of snow.

The ACR crew passes the miles swapping tales of steady runs with the clackety-clack of the wheels thumping out an irregular heartbeat to the swaying of the cars, of idyllic days with moose along the tracks, ducks drag-racing across a serene lake, of mosquitos and black flies so ferocious that they sometimes drive strong men to tears and send the bravest crying and clawing from the bush, of howling winds and temperatures plunging to fifty degrees below zero, and locomotives buried in a snow-clogged bank of track.

Those who venture the ACR line find their favorite stops, marking the progress by numbered telephone poles along the track: Agawa Canyon, Hawk Junction, Hearst. Only the adventurous choose Oba, population forty-three.

MILE 0: SAULT STE. MARIE

The baggage car is stacked high with supplies tagged for small grocers up the line, canoes, snowmobiles, lumber and roofing for cabin repairs, and even a rocking chair. I sense a different world that can be only imagined from the vibrant city of 83,000 affectionately called the Soo. The steel-producing city boasts shopping centers and exclusive salons, museums, the Soo Locks, which connect Lake Superior with the Saint Marys River and Lake Huron, gourmet restaurants, plush hotels, and busy streets with red double-decker buses straight from England.

All aboard! Excitement runs through the coaches. Faces crowd the windows. A jerk, and the train begins to move. Past a scrap yard. Past the International Bridge to Michigan. Past steel mills, houses, malls, and into the bush.

MILE 30: SEARCHMONT

The world has already changed. Farming and a small mining operation brought first settlers to the area in the 1890s. Lumbering and skiing keeps the village alive.

Growing accustomed to the fast-changing scenery, I dart back and forth across the car lest I miss anything. Lakes seem to spring into view before I am ready. Waterfalls catapulting down a cliff. Lake Superior tracing a blue line across the horizon as we ascend the peaks.

Algoma was the name originally suggested for Lake Superior. The word was coined by Henry Schoolcraft, Michigan's first Indian agent and friend of Henry Wadsworth Longfellow. Algoma was adopted as the name of the district in 1859.

MILE 48: OGIDAKI

At 2,184 feet above sea level, Ogidaki, which means "top of the hill" in the Ojibwa language, is Ontario's highest point.

MILE 80: BATCHAWANA

Meaning "narrows and swift water there", Batchawana refers to the dangerous river mouth at Lake Superior's Batchawana Bay.

Tracks swing like a horseshoe around the valley before crossing the Batchawana River bridge. Twice, it has been my destination, with my party dumped from the train to canoe south down a swift and twisting river to Lake Superior. Sleeping on sandbars. Portaging awesome waterfalls and shooting others only slightly less awesome.

MILE 92: MONTREAL RIVER

The fifteen hundred-foot curving trestle over the Montreal spans the river on spindly legs. On the downstream side, the land drops sharply for almost a hundred feet below the level of the trestle foundation, adding to the eerie height.

"Did you ever walk that trestle?" inquired an ACR engineer.

"No, but I crawled it one night," answered a seasoned brakeman.

MILE 102: FRATER

Railroad men tell of a raven that once followed freights for the twelve miles from Frater to the Agawa Canyon. For several years, rail crews threw bread to the raven as it followed along. The raven caught the morsels, stopped to bury them along the tracks, then flapped its wings hard to catch up and accompany the train down the canyon.

MILE 114: AGAWA CANYON

The train screams its way into the canyon, wheels no longer casually clacking and slapping against the rails. We brake to hold our course, iron screaming against iron, descending, snaking around curve after curve on our way to the canyon floor. Slowing at the Agawa River bridge, we chug past Bridal Veil Falls cascading along the track, past Black Beaver Falls on the left, and stop.

Agawa means "sheltered place" in Ojibwa, or "making for shelter," describing the mouth of Agawa River where it empties into Lake Superior or the shelter afforded the nomadic Indians by the steep granite and white quartz canyon walls.

Tourists step from the rain cars into serenity. They wander down paths to the waterfalls or up the steps that climb to an overlook perched on canyon walls. It is a time for picnics and short hikes, for wandering along the river where ripples gurgle quiet melodies. Children play. Couples stroll hand in hand. An old man in a floppy hat strings his fly rod to fish.

Then the conductor yells "All aboard!" During the winter, the Snow Train makes the same run, waterfalls frozen in ermine white, rivers silent, scenery sculpted postcard perfect. The train pauses in the canyon only long enough to switch directions. No picnics and leisurely strolls. Winter symphony played to the clacking of the wheels.

MILE 165: HAWK JUNCTION

It's the Hearst local from Hawk to the end of the line. Fishermen and hunters and a few seasoned adventurers find plenty of vacant seats in the coaches. A party of six shuffles a deck one more time and deals another hand as they wait for the Sand River stop, a game played on a woolen jacket stretched between their knees. They have three canoes in the baggage car, with equipment and supplies for the six days it takes to canoe down to Lake Superior's north shore where they spotted a car.

In the same baggage car are heaps of gear: backpacks, stovepipes for someone's camp, boat motors, bottles of propane for a trapper's cabin. A baggage man shifts the coffeepot on a hot plate and sorts mail into slots for delivery up the line.

Guitars strum as I push open the door of the car ahead.

College boys sing. A man in a red-checkered mackinaw sways to the train and off-key tune.

MILE 217: MOSHER

The occasional smell of a distant campfire sprinkles spices in the air. The country flattens. Rivers move more slowly. Maple, red oak, basswood, white elm and yellow birch give way to spruce, balsam and jack pine. Then swamp-loving aspen, tamarack and cedar take over.

A wizened old trapper rocks to the motion of the train, running callused fingers through his salt-and-pepper beard with tobacco stain at the corners. He tells how he once guided hunters and fishermen, keeping his trap line going at the same time.

"I had beaver pelts hanging from trees for miles around before I could get back and gather them all together."

MILE 245: OBA

Trainmen said nothing ever happened in Oba before the big policeman moved north to take over the old general store.

"I came out here for peace and quiet," the storekeeper declared.

Oba straddles the junction of the Algoma Central and Canadian National railways. Before the year-round road went through to Hearst in 1977, the village was accessible only by rail, except during winter months when the muskeg froze. "Town" was made up of two ancient hotels sagging in the muck, which alternately swapped a For Sale sign, Gailing's general store, liquor outlet, schoolhouse, scattering of railroad section houses, and a few hearty residents. Even the cemetery on the hill had a higher population than the town. When someone died, a preacher caught the Canadian National from Hornepayne forty miles to the west to conduct a funeral between trains. Townspeople dug the grave and tended to the burying after the preacher left, lowering the box with the fire hose that always hung ready in a cedar tree.

Day-by-day activity centered in the two hotel bars, with occasional excitement generated by a twenty-year-old Jerry Lewis movie shown at the schoolhouse.

Then Gailing came to town. His first six months were fairly quiet. Then one crisp autumn night, he climbed the stairs to his bedroom over the store. An oversized boxer called Judy sprawled at his feet; their snores and an occasional freight were the only sounds to interrupt the quiet of the bush.

At one A.M., the storekeeper was awakened by the tinkling of breaking glass. Kids playing down the tracks, he thought, and snored again. However, Gailing's store, forty miles from the nearest road and escape, was being robbed!

Shattered glass, a clutter of goods and a trail of Canadian bills greeted Gailing when he made his way down the stairs the next morning. Other evidence: expensive sleeping bags missing, along with parkas and liquor. Three strangers reportedly seen hopping off the midnight freight from Hornepayne. Three strangers kicked out of the hotel bar about one A.M. "One got lippy. I wouldn't serve them anymore," said the bartender.

Woodsmen said three strangers had showed up at their bush lumber camp at three A.M., giving away cartons of cigarettes and liquor. The chase was on, Oba style!

An hour before the first train was due, Gailing and sidekick Jack spotted a stranger walking along the tracks outside town. The suspect darted into the woods and swamps swollen by autumn rains. They gave chase, captured the robber, and turned him over for safekeeping to Big Tex, a bald, thick-chested trapper with huge hands who lived with a string of snarling sled dogs.

Tracking the other two through miles of tangled bush, Gailing and Jack finally lost them in the swamp. They headed back to Oba. Three miles outside the village, they heard the welcome rumble of the ACR.

"Flag it down," yelled Jack. "No use walking."

The broad-shouldered former policeman stood in the middle of the tracks, waving. The train roared closer.

"Keep waving," yelled Jack. "He'll blow his whistle when he sees you. The ACR stops for everybody."

The six-foot-three, 225-pound storekeeper didn't think he was that hard to spot! He waved until the last possible moment, then dived aside as the train roared past.

"I'll get the engineer for this," roared Jack. "I'll report this as soon as we're back in Oba."

In the village, the station agent grinned. "I told the engineer not to stop. Figured the robbers would try to flag the train."

Back at the store, Gailing called in the Ontario Provincial Police. When they stepped off the train, they were dressed in street uniforms, sadly equipped for a chase through the swamps.

With trains stopping for nobody and the nearest town miles through wet swamps, Gailing sat back and waited while the robbers tried to keep warm by lighting fires with his stolen money and kindling the flames with his expensive sleeping bags. Several days later, swarming mosquitoes drove them onto the tracks. Gailing's posse charged again. They ran down the robbers and tackled them into the muck. A well-dressed provincial police officer appeared and hauled them off to jail on the next train. A few years later the store burned down and Gailing moved south, but the memories linger still.

MILE 297: HEARST

End of the line, with little but muskeg and black flies to the north. A French-speaking market town with a Wild-West flavor. An agent for the Hudson's Bay Company still bought pelts. Tourists rode the ACR up for the night, and caught it south again with the morning light. They wandered down the street to the King Cafe or the Moonlight Grill, Northway Restaurant, Gulf Cafe, or settled for the chip stand—restaurants as varied as the populace. Some visitors were still around when a local woodsman led his horse into the bar of the Queens Hotel. When ordered from the premises, the owner argued that it was only a small horse.

66

"It ain't that," the bartender growled. "Horses shouldn't be drunk before nine o'clock at night."

FROM HEARST SOUTH

Frost turned the rails to sparkling silver the morning friend Tom Buchkoe and I jumped the southbound freight at Hearst. Sun streaked down the tracks licking up the dew, except where it crept into the shadows of the station and the empty cars waiting on the sidings.

Selin the freight conductor and his assistant Bain swung onto the caboose that ACR men call the "van." Selin had invited me to ride the freight two years earlier, and had finally cleared it with the line only minutes before we climbed aboard. Freight hoppers have all but disappeared, he said, along with steam engines.

It is an all-day run by freight to Hawk Junction 130 miles south, so we stowed our baggage under the short bunks. We climbed up to the cupola while the train cleared the Hearst yard.

Whistles blasted. Cars jerked. Then came the rhythmic sway and clacking clatter of wheels slapping against the rails.

Hoboes, I thought with a grin, as Selin handed up steaming cups of coffee freshly perked on the van stove.

"Toast and eggs coming up," Selin said.

He balanced slices of bread on a homemade toaster and watched heat rise through the holes punched in the bottom of a peaches can inverted over the flame. Bain was already dropping carrots into a stew simmering for our lunch. The men talked back and forth with the engineers, tallying cars for the next stop. "You'll ride the engine out of Newaygo," Selin said.

The bush seems closer when viewed from a swaying freight; it seems friendlier, free, and wild. Orange-coated hunters waved from along the tracks, waiting for a nearsighted moose to venture across the clearing. Old-timers sat outside their shacks to toast in the last of autumn rays. They waved as we lumbered noisily past, then slumped back into their toasting before winter spread its chill across the bush.

At Newaygo, Tom and I ran down the cinders and climbed aboard the engine. The hot, oily smell of machinery mixed with morning air as we led the line of cars down the track, whistle trumpeting our approach at crossings. At noon, we ran back down the track to join Selin and Bain over stew.

Hawk Junction came too soon for me. We swung down from the van and crossed the train yard. As cinders crunched beneath my feet, I felt the pangs that still haunt me every time I hear the whistle of a train: clatter on the rails, sway behind a long line of cars, toast browned over a peaches can, sipping coffee from a cupola, the smell of hot engine oil, stray cinders in my eye. Hobo blues!

10

BESS

BESS CAPAGROSSA IS ONE of those feisty women with a keen wit and sharp tongue, which she uses to thinly disguise a heart of gold.

She draws up a stool, leans her arms on the counter of her Superior Hotel in Grand Marais, Michigan, and watches the world go by. Graying hair curls like a cap to her head. She purses her thin lips, brushes a hand to adjust big glasses and turns her round face to greet a customer who picks up a paper, drops coins on the counter and leaves.

Outside, a passing truck slows. The driver reads the sign posted in the window and moves on. Bess smiles.

The wind picks up, rattling the last autumn leaves to the ground. Across the street beyond the Lumberjack Bar, the grocery store and gas station, Bess can see waves of Lake Superior splashing against the break wall.

At one place or another, Bess has watched the world from behind counters for most of her life – bars, restaurants, and her own five-stool soda fountain at the hundred-year-old hotel. She has carved her niche in life to the backdrop of this fishing and tourist village of about four hundred population, a niche that changes with the mood of the seasons, a niche made comfortable with friends who drop in and the wind and water and the trees outside. Bess is never lonely.

"I go to sleep with the wind in the trees and the splash of water against the shore," she said. "I couldn't live without water."

The quaint village began as a fishing village and harbor of refuge for early voyageurs. It is now the eastern gateway to Pictured Rocks National Lakeshore, with a snug natural harbor, agate beaches mixed with secluded coves of squeaky sand, and the towering 85-foot-high AuSable Dunes stacked on top of the 275-foot-high glacial deposits of the Grand Sable Banks.

Summers, tourists come to climb the dunes, to splash in the waters of Grand Sable Lake, follow the wooded path to Sable Falls, to fish the area's lakes and streams. Winters, tourists return on snowmobiles and cross-country skis to enjoy the scenery all over again, draped in a mantle of white.

When her stepfather Grumpy brought Bess and her mother to the village, it was populated by fishermen and lumbermen. Fishermen had ready markets for their catches, and other captains catered to tourists.

The railroads that hauled the tall timbers from the forest had already gone when Grumpy moved back home. But Bess can remember the old-time lumberjacks who stayed in the woods for six months at a time. They would come to town with big rolls of bills tied with rubber bands, and head for the nearest bar. "They would sit there until the bartender kicked them out to close, and they would come right back when the doors opened the next day."

She recalled Grumpy's stepfather Big John with the huge hands who promised her and her brother gifts when he came. Her brother ended up with a fancy pair of high-cut boots with a pocket and knife in the side. Before he could buy such a gift for Bess, the magnetic pull of the bars grew too strong to resist. He bought them a bag of candy and sent them home to their

mother. As usual, Grumpy paid somebody to take Big John back
to the woods when his roll of money was gone.

Homefolks ran the stores and saloons then. Bess and the hotel
are the last of the family businesses, as old-timers move on and
strangers move in. She feels the difference. She says it seems like
businesses are continually for sale, continually changing hands.

Seems that the only things that stay the same are the changing seasons, the wind, the forest and the lake that refuses to be tamed.

Winter nights, Bess turns on the outside light which illuminates her doorway and watches the snowflakes fall. "When you are raised here, you learn to appreciate the air, sky and water more than other people do. I love it so much that I never want to go anywhere."

Villagers stop in for newspapers and sundries. The phone rings and someone inquires about a room. "They're clean," she tells the caller. "But the bathrooms are down the hall. I don't want you to come all the way up here and be disappointed." The caller reserves a room.

Nine upstairs rooms in the rambling old hotel with old-West facade rent from twelve to fifteen dollars a night. Single rooms go for eight dollars when booked for several nights. They are furnished with a bed, chair and chest, with a pole and several hangers in the corner for clothes. Neighbors say Bess dries her sheets outdoors, that you can smell their freshness when you turn back the soft chenille spreads and blankets at night.

The Superior Hotel has no private baths, no televisions or telephones in the rooms. There is not even a telephone listing in the directories.

"When telephones came to Grand Marais, we had the first exchange, with eight extensions on our line. Our ring was two F four, or two shorts and four longs on the party line. Afterward, when the telephone company brought in more lines, we had one for the hotel and one for us. They were going to charge double for the hotel, so Dad just kept our family phone. It's been that way ever since. Besides, I don't need the extra listing. Folks who come know where I am."

Bess pauses as a car pulls up to the hotel. The driver peers out his window, spots her sign, and drives away. Bess says the driver is a friend who knows to watch for the sign on minor holidays. When the mail doesn't run up the twenty-five-mile highway from Seney, folks have to wait for the milk truck to deliver the newspapers. Still, delivery is better than the old days when the mailman started out for Seney on a cold winter day with a pint in his pocket. At the halfway house, he shared steaming bowls of soup with the mailman from Seney, and hiked back again.

Her father, Alfred "Grumpy" Lundquist, bought the old Pippin Hotel in 1939 and changed its name to Superior. Grumpy was born in the village of Grand Marais. When he was young, "like so many, he jumped the rails." He ended up in Alberta, Canada, where he met Bess's mother Mabel. Mabel was from London's dock district. After the district was blown apart during World War II, Mabel, her sister, and a friend booked passage on a ship for Canada.

"She never went back except once for Christmas, even for a visit. Her relatives would come here to see her."

Bess was born in Toronto. Her face darkens to a frown when she speaks of this.

"Mother never told me that Grumpy was my stepfather. A relative had to tell me," she said. "After so many years had passed, I wouldn't ask her about it. I wanted to know but I was stubborn. I have a lot of English in me, too."

Bess was three years old when the family moved to Grand Marais. Grumpy ran a seasonal charter boat for fishermen, the Attaboy. He trolled in his later years. He marked all his spoon fishing lures with the name Grumpy. When he inadvertently snagged a commercial net, he cut his line and left the spoons. In the fall when the fishermen gathered in their nets, they harvested Grumpy's spoons and brought them in.

Grumpy and Mabel opened a restaurant, the village's first. "Before that, salesmen had to buy cheese, crackers and baloney at the general store. After we had been opened for a while, everybody thought we were getting rich, and more restaurants started up."

She recalls growing up in the area where fishing and lumbering were the primary industries. Kids spent free hours sledding down the big hills that surround the bay. On summer afternoons, Grumpy would load his growing family in the old Model T with the top off, and drive out along the shore road to the vacant Grand Marais Hardwood Mill. "He would stop at the door and let us kids yell and listen to our echo."

There were streams to fish, waterfalls, and the Grand Sable

Dunes to climb, now part of the Pictured Rocks National Lakeshore. "Kids had so much to do, we would often ignore our homework," she recalled with a faint smile.

Then, as now, some winter mornings Bess would wake to icebergs all over the harbor, bobbing on the current, sharp spires pointing skyward. Temperatures drop and the eerie silence comes, water sealed to silence under the ice with barely a rumble until a wind change shifts them from the harbor and into deep open water, or spring comes again.

Bess rambles on about the seasons, the lake, village life. More village folks push open the hotel door. Most linger to chat. Conversation drifts to the past. Someone mentions Pickle Meldrum.

"I remember him as a kid," another says. "I remember him feeding his mutt a hot dog on a string, then pulling it back up and feeding it to him again."

They laugh at the old familiar story.

"Wasn't he the kid who took the motor off his mother's sewing machine to make a milk shake?"

"Yeah. The glass jar broke and milk went all over the place." Someone chuckles.

Later, Bill Madore stops in from the Lakeview bed and breakfast inn across the street. They chat about the weather, the holiday with no mail delivery from the post office, and the sign in the window. He buys a pack of cigarettes and leaves.

"He's new in town, but he's nice. He's friendly. He and his wife help out," Bess says.

Bess rings up the sale on the shiny old National cash register.

"It tallies up to $4.99," she comments. "I don't remember having any other register in this place except this one that Dad bought secondhand."

Bess hasn't always lived in Grand Marais. As a young woman, she married a serviceman and moved away. "I lived in Florida, South Carolina, Wisconsin, and finally in Brooklyn, but I never found any place I like better than Grand Marais."

When her marriage failed, she came home with her four children, including twins. She went to work helping Grumpy and Mabel in the hotel. Mabel was cooking for the dining room where meals were served to guests and friends; they gathered family-style around two big tables. The general public ate in the main parlor. Although the restaurant has been closed for years, the big tables are still there. Instead of big trout dinners including soup, pie and coffee, tables hold a variety of Bess's projects such as balls of yarn for knitting and other crafts. In the front windows, wrought iron ice cream chairs and tables where visitors were once served hold Bess's many potted plants.

No room in the hotel exhibits family ties more strongly than the parlor area off the entrance way. The small lobby is crowded with upholstered chairs, more plants, and an upright piano lined with fading family photos. Other photos hang a bit askew on the walls. A stairway leads to the second floor. Here, in the big room stored with memories with a lock on the door, Bess raised her family.

Upstairs halls and downstairs lobby seem to echo of a younger Bess, with four children and grandparents underfoot and guests in all the rooms. One imagines grandparents in front of the television listening to Lawrence Welk, grandchildren in the kitchen running the blender to create static on the screen in hopes that they will turn to another channel, Bess working the village bars for extra money, and going in at two A.M. when the bars close to snatch some sleep before work in the hotel begins again. There were once twenty-one bars in the village, but by the time Bess moved home, count was down to four.

"Over a twenty-three-year period, I worked in them all. I never pushed drinks," she said. "I went to church all the time I was tending bars. I was careful. I watched my reputation. I wanted to set a good example for my children."

She never remarried. "I made such a bad judgment the first time that with my luck, I was afraid I'd do it again. And I didn't think it was fair to the children to give them another father. Besides, over the years I got bossy."

Bess's sister-in-law Jean Lundquist pushes open the door. Like other villagers, she helps herself at the candy counter and drops coins in the register. The two women visit, catching up on the news, reminiscing about the old days. Something reminds them of Mrs. McNally with all her rings and the time she mistook

Alfie's look-alike cat Willie for her own. Alfie, Jean's son, was going out of town, and Willie needed a sitter.

"That little snot! I should have known he had something tucked under his coat," Jean said.

Alfie showed up at her door, asking his mother to care for Willie while he was away. During the weekend, Willie somehow disappeared. A neighbor found Willie dead in the road, apparently struck by a passing car. Jean said she would bury poor unfortunate Willie the following day. However, next morning Willie was gone.

Later she heard that the McNallys from the General Store had found the cat. Thinking it was theirs, grieving Mrs. McNally had taken a forty-dollar jacket off the store racks and wrapped Willie snugly inside. They took him to their shaded backyard, dug a grave, and tearfully said their farewells to Willie, jacket and all.

Several nights later, after the McNallys had closed the store, their errant cat repented and came scratching at their back window. Mrs. McNally's rings trembled. She screamed. She thought she was being haunted by a cat-ghost!

Although the McNally's got their cat back, Jean and Alfie loved thinking about poor Willie wrapped in that forty-dollar jacket, sleeping peacefully in the McNally's backyard.

Jean heads for home. The telephone rings with another reservation. Bess jots the information on a pad. "Snowmobilers," she said. "There won't be a vacant room in town during the Christmas holidays."

A customer drives up and rattles open the door.

"He didn't read my sign," she said in feigned disgust. "There's no paper today. I post a sign in the window to save them the trouble of coming in, but they come anyway."

The man walks to the counter and slaps down his coins.

"Didn't you read my sign?" Bess says. "I don't know why you need a newspaper. You can't read!"

The customer stalks back through the door without his newspaper. Bess grins. Then she leans on the counter and watches the wind pushing whitecaps past the break wall, past the lighthouse on the point, and across the harbor to sigh and splatter themselves against the rocky beach, recarving the shoreline inch by inch.

"It's gonna do what it wants," she said, nodding toward Superior. "You're not gonna change it."

Like Bess.

11

YOUNG'S GENERAL STORE

A SIGN ON YOUNG'S General Store in Wawa, Ontario, proclaims, "There is no other place like this, so this must be the place." Inside, customers and visitors discover why.

Bill Young is perched on the top of an empty milk can like a mischievous leprechaun. He speaks softly, almost in a whisper, yet the gleam in his eye gave a hint of tales to be told. He insisted that business is different in the bush where "it takes more nerve than dollars to operate." That is where he sometimes runs afoul of the law.

Unless the twenty-eight-foot-tall, two-ton statue of the Wawa wild goose that stands at the Welcome Center down the highway has made tracks again, Young has kept his tricks in check for quite a while. However, he promised the goose will walk again.

Young's General Store is a weather-worn collection of buildings that houses almost everything a person ever thought of buying. Tacked on walls, stacked in aisles, piled in and on showcases, are bear traps and boxing gloves, spices, cast-iron skillets, eggs in open flats, lanterns hanging from the ceiling, an old treadle sewing machine, snowshoes, hard candy, scrub boards, horse collars, cookies from a tin sold by the pound. He sells grain from open bags: barley, buckwheat, beans, peas. Reach in and help yourself. Or fork a sour pickle from the open barrel that stands at the front door.

"Customers get entertainment while they shop," he says. "People tie it to the good old days and old pleasant memories."

During Young's youth, his grandfather operated a store east of Sault Ste. Marie. Young thought it might be fun to be a storekeeper, but he wanted a store with an old-fashioned air. The animals came by accident.

His first store was a twenty-by-twenty-eight-foot structure, which he opened with an investment of seventy dollars for taxes and goods on consignment. "I bought a model cottage from the Indians, hauled it over with a school bus and stocked up," he said.

When summer came, weeds grew rapidly in the rocky front yard, weeds that Young had neither time nor inclination to mow. He decided to invest in a goat, which he hoped would keep the grass clipped short. Trouble started when he answered an advertisement for a goat and the owner said, "Why don't you borrow my ass, too?"

Young did, and was soon charged with keeping a goat and a donkey at a business establishment. In answer to a complaint, "police came and took my goat and donkey while my wife Anita was home alone," Young says.

On his way to bail out his animals, Young made a detour to the local newspaper and placed an advertisement in the Lost and Found. He saved the clipping: "Someone got my GOAT and took my ASS (donkey). Anyone knowing whereabouts of same please notify Bill at Young's Gift and Bait Shop. Suspect believed to be driving Police Cruiser."

Business picked up as everyone came to see what the trouble was all about. Young says the advertisement and the resulting rush of customers is probably what prompted the visit from police. However, by the time they arrived, the incident had landed in newspapers as far south as Toronto.

"The police learned they couldn't have two charges on one summons, so they dropped the goat," he said.

With the donkey trial set, Young renamed his animal "Chief." He contended that Chief was a mule. Defense was that a mule was part horse, which was legal in Wawa.

Meanwhile, more publicity was in the making. Young insists that he thought it only proper that he photograph his donkey-mule-horse. He drove to police headquarters and asked to borrow the police chief's uniform hat for the pose. The chief walked in during negotiations and reclaimed his hat in a huff. "He didn't have much of a sense of humor."

Young said he had other advertisements ready if he had lost his case, where he insisted that if he had to go to jail, so did the mule.

Crown experts were called to Wawa to testify on the animal's classification. Charges for keeping animals at a business establishment were dropped, according to newspapers, when "those persons concerned couldn't distinguish between a donkey, ass, mule and so on."

Then there was excitement at the store over geese, a bear, fifteen hundred chickens that didn't sell, "so I traded for hogs," and the big row over the pickle barrel.

Ontario Department of Health officials did not take to open pickle barrels which they considered unsanitary. "Your theme of an old-fashioned general store is good, but you've let your business run away with you," they said.

While insisting that his salesmanship was not prompted by mischief, Young somehow held on to his pickle barrel.

Then near-disaster struck. At four A.M. on April 4, 1979, a seventy-pound Husky name Tonka woke the Youngs from deep sleep. The store attached to their living quarters was in flames. Almost everything was destroyed. They started to rebuild with "very little insurance and not much time. We were up and into the store the last of June, except for windows."

Young opened the store for business, trying to complete the building between customers. Plastic sheets were secured at night. Police moved in. They said the store was technically closed until it was completed and all inspections passed. Orders were to padlock.

Young fastened a padlock in the plastic, and kept selling. Police padlocked the door, so Young rolled up the plastic over the window every morning and conducted business through the opening. Police threatened to board up everything, so Young got ready with another newspaper ad: "Chain saw opening coming up."

Sales flourished.

"I had TV coverage lined up from the Soo if they jailed me," he said. "The police were pulling rank. When the junior guy on the force was told he had to arrest me, he threatened to quit. It was cute."

Somehow frontier justice prevailed with everybody saving face, and further confrontation was avoided.

Then there was the matter of the Wawa goose. Young admits to nothing; he only relates that huge goose tracks were found one morning in the dawning light, leading from the statue, across the Welcome Center's parking area, and down the highway. A highway crew was sent from the Soo to paint over the tracks of the wayward nocturnal goose. That night, a phantom crew went out and painted tracks a second time, with the addition of shiny, sparkling glass beads sprinkled into wet paint.

Perched on his milk can, Young pokes at the fire in the big cast-iron stove and glances furtively across the store before speaking softly, nodding knowingly. "It's going to happen again soon," he says. "It creates employment."

The Wawa goose never walked again. Bill Young died in 1988.

12

MARGE

EVENING SUN STRETCHES LONG across the tidy yard, pushing the shadows of the cottage into irregular angles – like a carnival house of mirrors – on the slope that leads to Clear Creek. Pushing the giant elm with its yellowing leaves to mingle as one with the woodshed where the woman keeps her traps, duck decoys and canoe. Pushing the trailing shadow of the woman herself into a rippling finger, which flows along after her as she makes her way down the path from the truck parked in the drive.

Marge Moll shoulders her twenty-gauge and pats the partridge in her pack. "Nice wing shot," she murmurs. Reg taught her that shot years ago, soon after their marriage.

"Reg would have been proud of that one, old gal," she adds. Talking to herself, to the wind, or to no one in particular is not unusual for Marge. It is a habit she picked up years ago as she tromped through the woods. She has talked to ruffed grouse, woodcock and other game birds when the forests around Bruce Crossing in Michigan's western Upper Peninsula turned ablaze with autumn colors, to ducks and geese, to the animals she trapped, to deer and even fish. It came from her hours of prowling the trails alone, with wild creatures her only companions. "Not bad company," she said, walking toward her cabin beside the road.

Bruce Crossing is a village of about two hundred people equidistant between main branches of the Ontonagon River system. Attire of the villagers who gather daily around the big wooden round table at Tulppo's Restaurant reflects each gaming season: hunting vests, bright orange great coats, winter mackinaws, swampers, hip waders. Hats run from canvas flattops brimmed with feathery trout flies to helmets and snug-over-the-ears rabbit hunters' chukes, or knitted stocking caps.

Spring softens the surrounding forests in mid-April with the greening of the tamarack in the swamps, lime-green, with tiny needles prickling the bare limbs. Suddenly spring is joined by leaves no bigger than a mouse's ear all across the aspen groves, with arbutus sending forth sweet perfume from the ground where the sun first warms the forest floor. Marge watches it all, keeping a keen eye out for the blossoming of wild berries. She will return with pail in hand for the autumn harvest of blackberries, raspberries and blueberries, with special trips for pin cherries for her jellies. Marge is careful of sugarplum trees. This is where she is most likely to meet up with bears. "I pussyfoot around the bears," she said.

She loves the woodsy smells, which are already changing to a spicy hint of autumn across Clear Creek. Leaves will soon be gone. She has already gathered many specimens of the fiery maple, which will slowly dry to fine parchment on her windowsill, their fire waned to the color of burgundy wine before the season comes around again.

Another sprig sits on her kitchen table with the homespun cloth reflected in the crystal vase. It is, in fact, a homespun kitchen, with cupboard stocked full of jellies from her wild berries and homemade bread in the freezer alongside wild game. All prepared between seasons.

"Come fishing or bird season, I ain't cookin' no more," she invariably announces to friends who drop in.

The outdoorswoman stays busy from dawn until the evening hours, puttering in her kitchen, sampling the outdoors, doing whatever pleases her. She withstood a bout with cancer to bounce back feeling young again, her favorite woodland paths light and springy beneath her step.

Tonight, the stream makes a gurgling sound off in the shadows. But is there something more? Sensing that there might be, Marge turns to glance over her shoulder, raising her head slightly to squint through the thick glasses that like to slip down her long, classical nose. The trail is empty.

Her thoughts turn back to Reg, and a smile spreads across her weather-lined face. "Must have been that wing shot that brought him back so close this evening," she said. She missed Reg profoundly after he died in 1971. They had shared the woods together: Reg the teacher, Marge his willing pupil.

There it is again—the near-imperceptible sound, a rustle, a presence sensed in the dimming light. Then something brushes gently against her foot. Startled, Marge looks down. Padding along beside her, dogging her steps, strolls a skunk! There are two animals of the woods that Marge has never taken to—bears and skunks. Both have odors not to her liking: the unmistakable odor often left by her companion here and the one she describes as "piggy" left by bears.

"Who do you think I am, Grizzly Adams?" Marge chides in a loud, raspy voice. "Now what in the world would Reg have done with you?" If the skunk knows, it isn't saying.

Reginald Moll: imposing woodsman over six feet tall, fifteen years her senior when they met, fifteen years ahead of her in his knowledge of the outdoors. Reg got an early start prowling the woods during his teen years around Kenton. His father, a physician, tried to interest him in higher education such as chosen by his younger brother, but Reg defiantly stuck to field and stream.

"All he wanted to do was fish and hunt and trap with a little guiding on the side, and that's all he ever did worth doing," Marge said.

In the mid-1930s, Reg was in charge of predator control at the Seney Wildlife Refuge. Later, he came to Bruce Crossing as a state trapper, along with cronies John Polvi and Mike Luckaw. Those two called Reg "Spike," as most other folks did.

"I wasn't nothin' but a kid then," Marge remembers aloud as

the skunk darts across her lawn. "Before we got married, I usually didn't pay much attention to him, except to laugh. They always had the fun, those three. Made everybody laugh and feel good. Had as much fun as a bunch of outlaws."

Marge laughs, remembering, all the time slapping her leg, which makes the intruding skunk run faster and head in a straight, determined line for the safety of the nearby woodshed.

Reg's early life had not been too different from hers. She had grown up on a farm, milking cows and helping out. But she always found time for fishing. In her early twenties, she cooked for the lumberjacks in her father's lumber camp. Besides cooking, there wasn't much extra to do. Boards were so far apart on the cookhouse floor that the dirt fell straight through, so there was little need for a broom.

Marge whiled away some of her spare time by setting a trap for a pesky weasel that had become an unwelcome visitor. When that proved fruitful, she began to set out a regular trap line for other critters. And she frequently took off to fish on the nearby streams.

Even after she married Reg in 1955, she still stuck with her spinning gear. Reg kidded her as he reached for his fly rod, but never bothered to instruct her. Then one day Reg was guiding a party from Milwaukee and a friend felt sorry for Marge, who was trailing far behind on catch. That friend handed Marge an extra fly rod and taught her the finer points. By day's end, Marge was keeping up, fish for fish. She has been keeping up ever since, especially with brook trout and bluegill.

"Nothin' like bluegills on a fly rod with a popper," she said in the gently falling night. Even the old skunk heard her and peeked out from behind his corner of the shed.

The senior ladies around Bruce Crossing have been taking careful note of the days Marge heads after bluegills. "Good eating," they tell her, while complaining that they are too old to fish. Marge will show them next summer. She has laid careful plans for those old gals. She plans to load them into her pickup and head for Bond Falls. There, on the flowage dam above the cascade of falls, she will set up stools, give each a fishing rod and turn them loose. "Ain't no reason they can't keep fishing if they want to," she said. "Just might need a little help."

The women wonder at Marge with near-jealous awe, the way she takes off for the woods alone: by snowmobile or snowshoes in winter to run her trap lines, on foot or in her truck the rest of the year, letting the seasons dictate her mode of travel and accessories.

"I throw my canoe into the back of my truck and bang! I'm gone," she likes to say.

Marge's favorite jaunt involves the pursuit of brook trout along her special stretch of the Ontonagon where the ripples curve around a low island just short of a rustic cabin, with a sugarplum that attracted the bear. The spot is near where she returns in winter with her traps.

Reg taught her well of trapping, starting with her first query about some mink tracks. She was running his grandson's line the day she grew curious about mink. "How do you trap mink, Reg?" she had asked. Reg not only spent days instructing her, but sent along his friend Johnny to see how she was doing. She was proud the day Johnny found a coyote in her trap.

Marge normally throws a variety of equipment into her truck, since she can never be sure of the outdoor offerings on any given day. Even during bird season, she lays a few traps, "just enough to keep me out of mischief." That takes her right into deer season, and she always has a good idea where a big buck may be waiting.

It isn't downing the buck that counts to Marge, any more than the landing of another fish. What's really important is being in a position to do so. "Something different happens out there every day," she said. "I even dream about the woods at night."

Perhaps the skunk senses her reverie. There he is peeking out again, taking a tentative step in her direction.

"Skunk, this place ain't big enough for both of us. I told you my name ain't Adams." Marge raises her shotgun and, in a sudden glow that precedes full darkness, takes steady aim as the skunk makes a hasty retreat.

It is the ever-changing of the woods that attracts her, that pulls her back day after day: changing colors, flowers, birds on the move, berries, smells.

Smell? Is that a "piggy" smell? "Not now, bear," she said. "I can only reckon with one of you at a time." The odor she always stood wary of recedes and then is gone.

It vanished faster tonight than it had three weeks ago. The river had been perfect that day, hugging her waders and swirling around the small boulders on the pebbled bottom as she cast time and again. She waded on, savoring the sunny afternoon, when suddenly she detected the piggy smell nearby.

"I wonder if that's a bear," she said loudly. "You dern fool, don't answer yourself now," she whispered, "you'd better pussyfoot out of here." Her fly rod aloft, Marge splashed for cover.

The bear did some pussyfooting of his own when Marge dropped her creel and scattered fern-covered trout along the trail. Breathless moments later, she had claimed the safety of her truck.

Marge had drawn a bead on the skunk. The shot must be just right. The light will soon be gone and her favorite pair of waders are hanging inside the woodshed, well within skunk range.

"Gotta bring them inside tomorrow," she said. "Be too cold soon. Gotta be careful or I'll be running around like Reg's old pal Mike."

She had marveled at Mike, who wore wool socks and ankle-top tennies through all seasons. Marge suspected he stuck to tennies to mask his scent in the woods. She preferred hip waders, adding more socks to keep her toes warm. Reg teased that she never took off those waders all year long, fishing in them during spring and summer and trapping in them during winter.

"I should have asked old Mike why he always wore those shoes," Marge said. "He was certainly around enough, after my wild game dinners."

It is well into her dinner hour, and Marge thinks of those dinners now. Reg, with his craving for her homemade bread and wild raspberry jam. And turtle fricassee. "Cooked just like chicken," she said. "So good you could throw the chicken away and never miss it." She'd gladly tromp five miles right now to bring home a turtle, if not for her preoccupation with the skunk "pussyfooting behind my woodshed."

She waits, squinting down her gun barrel as the skunk draws back into concealment, only to peek out again curiously. Marge thinks of all the different animals she has trapped over the years: mink, muskrat, beaver, coyote, fox. She questions the fabled intelligence of the fox.

"Old fox, he ain't nothin'," she said. "Coyote is the sly one. He is a cagey sonofagun, but don't look at his little ones or you'll go sentimental."

It is now impossible for her to make out the skunk's eyes in the growing dusk, but she feels his steady gaze. She wonders where he had been heading before she came along. Home?

"Now don't go sentimental, ole gal," she said. There he is again, checking her out. Why doesn't he make a run for it and head for the shrubs along the creek? She isn't about to give chase.

"You dern fool, why don't you pussyfoot yourself out of here?"

She lowers the gun and shrugs, then her laughter fills the night air. "I can't shoot you now, but I hope somebody else does."

Marge opens her cottage door and pussyfoots inside to dinner waiting in the oven. She pulls out the chair beside the window with its sprig of autumn leaves. For the sake of memories, she sets out a saucer and places on it a slice of homemade bread thick with butter and wild raspberry jam.

13

THE LEGISLATOR PLAYS
THE SPOONS

H E WAS PART OF a unique breed referred to as the U.P.
mafia. For the twenty years the white-haired man with the
wild impish eyebrows and big grin served in the Michigan
House of Representatives, they said his occupation was raising
hell. On the House floor in Lansing, Russell "Rusty" Hellman
from Dollar Bay screamed and yelled and moaned, waved his
hands and pounded fists until opponents shook their heads in
despair and said, "Enough, give it to him! We're not going to
listen to that all night long."

In the end, Rusty always allowed his opponents to save face.

Downstate politicians called them the "U.P. boys," legislators
from Michigan's Upper Peninsula, which included Rusty,
Dominic "Jake" Jacobetti of Negaunee, Joe Mack from Ironwood
and others. And side by side with Rusty was a perky little
woman who declared she hated politics, but fought for the U.P.
beside him all the way. Together, the U.P. mafia created a unique

brand of politics that is slowly disappearing as they retire one by one.

Rusty came upon the political scene with fire in his throat and a grudge in his heart. The U.P.'s Tip O'Neill was an unlikely candidate from the beginning. He was battling a frustrating stutter and a burning hatred for his seventh grade teacher who had made a practice of ridiculing him and his speech impediment in front of classmates. And there was the incident of the ice scrapers and brooms.

His mother and father, John and Hilda Hellman, had emigrated from Finland in search of the legendary American streets of gold. "Dad was disappointed when he discovered that streets were not of gold, they weren't even paved. Then he learned that if he ever wanted the streets paved, he had to help pay for it."

The second youngest of twelve children, Rusty grew up on the same street where he now lives in Dollar Bay along the Portage Canal of the Keweenaw Peninsula. His parents rushed to become American citizens. By example to their children, they instilled a pride in the political process and respect for authority.

"They never missed an election and its opportunity to vote. My mother would get dressed up to go to vote. It meant something to her," Rusty says.

The Hellmans were especially impressed with Justice of the Peace Dunston, who lived in a big colonial-type red house across the street. "When our parents saw Mr. Dunston coming, we weren't even allowed out of our yard. That's the respect they had for law and authority."

Rusty first felt the pull of politics while attending the eleventh grade at Dollar Bay High School. He and his buddies built a skating rink that winter. They cleared a road to the rink, flooded a vacant lot, scraped it smooth and swept it clear of falling snowflakes. They scrounged lumber, built a warming shack, added an old barrel stove for heat, and cut wood to fire it up.

It was in the middle of the depression. Because the community was using the rink and Rusty and his buddies were doing all the work, Rusty proposed the idea of asking for a

donation of scrapers and brooms from Osceola Township Supervisor Bergen, who was also superintendent of Calumet & Hecla Mining Company, the area's largest employer. The guys agreed. As they walked the five miles to Tamarack and the mining company offices, the guys further agreed that since it was Rusty's idea, he should be their spokesman.

"Abraham Lincoln Bergen was a conservative Republican through and through, a single-tunnel Republican," Rusty said. "He was a soft-spoken man. But when I finished my pitch, he shook his finger at me, and said, 'Young man, do you think the world owes you a living? Is this your ambition in life, to stand on the side of the road asking for alms? Are you going to be a parasite on society all your life? Young man, don't you believe in private enterprise and doing for yourself? What would this nation be if all of our young people had your attitude?'"

Rusty tells the story with shaking finger and fire still burning in his eyes. Then he leans back in his chair, remembering.

"You see, I was insulted. It was an insult to my parents who worked so hard. An insult to my father who worked as a copper refiner in the Quincy smelter and my mother who got dressed up to go vote."

He was quiet, remembering, then turned on the "Rusty fire" again.

"I shook my finger, too, and said, 'Mr. Bergen, someday I'll have your job.' And I spun on my heels and off we went."

Walking back to Dollar Bay, the boys were halfway home when "the C & H truck spun by with a load of brooms and scrapers. They were leaning on the door of our shack when we got there."

Rusty never lost sight of his commitment to run as Osceola township supervisor, a job Bergen held for twenty-six years. When he reached the age of twenty-one, he ran against Bergen and beat him by forty-seven votes. "And I couldn't even vote for him. I wasn't old enough," said his wife Edith.

Soon after the confrontation with Bergen over the scrapers and brooms, the gas station across the street from the Hellman home went up for sale. Rusty wanted that station! He approached the local oil distributor with a proposal: if he would help Rusty with financing to buy the station, Rusty would sell his gas.

The dealer was nervous; Rusty was still a senior in high school. He went to Rusty's father.

"Our parlor was used only for special occasions, and they went into the parlor," Rusty recalled in awe.

The dealer asked Mr. Hellman how much money he intended to put into the venture. None, he had none.

"If you were me, would you trust this kid for the deal?"

"Yes, I would."

Rusty got the station and the oil dealer held the mortgage. He ran back and forth between school, the station and home. Five years later, he cleared the deed. Rusty still owns that little station. Pumps are gone, but the little building is still there, full of shovels from ground breakings, full of plaques, awards and recognitions from his years in Lansing. His office files are there, in thirty-eight black boxes. Several libraries requested the files as historical documents, libraries at Michigan Technological University at Houghton, Michigan State Library at Lansing and others. Rusty went through one of the files, trying to decide.

"There are too many lives in these files, too many personal things, letters from people poring their hearts out to their legislator. I don't want strangers reading these stories. They are too personal. These people trusted me."

As the political fires in him grew, Rusty met Edith. A carload of youths from Dollar Bay drove up the road to a dance at Electric Park.

"I was a cocky high school senior, an upgoing guy, egotistical, argumentive, obnoxious. You've got to be all those things to be a politician," he says with a chuckle and wide grin. "There was this luscious young gal from Calumet on the other side of the room, looking at me, wanting to dance with me."

Edith objects quietly. "I was looking at the guy next to you."

"After two dances, I thought, 'This is not bad!' I asked to take her home,and she said she was going home with her brother." He followed the short blonde outside. Taking hold of her arm, he said, "Come on. My car is over here."

That night, Rusty learned that Edith is not one to be pushed around. She turned toward him, clenching her fists. "You don't understand. I said I was going home with my brother."

After high school, Rusty left to seek his fortune in Detroit. After a strike, he came home and went to work for a Dodge and

Plymouth garage, selling cars on commission and four gallons of gasoline a day. And he waited for his twenty-first birthday when he could run against Mr. Bergen.

One Mothers Day, an older neighbor asked to be driven to church in Rusty's car. "I could either go in church with her, or drive up the road and see if that cute gal was still around. I decided to go see Edith."

They enjoyed the day so much that Rusty made a date for Thursday night. "But Thursday was such a long way off, so I went back Monday. Thursday was still a long way off, so I went back Tuesday and Wednesday. Her mother was getting suspicious."

Edith interrupted. "My uncle and aunt had driven into the yard as we were leaving, and saw who I was with. They had met him while visiting a friend in the hospital." She waved her arms in circles, drawing a web. "They started telling me what a nice person he was and all that good stuff, just tangling me in there. By the time Thursday came around, I didn't tell Rusty I already had a date for the dance. As we left, there came my date in a red convertible. I just waved at him and we kept going."

Rusty and Edith were married in 1938. Soon they wanted a house. At an auction, Rusty bid on an old school building. The low bidder was a wrecker from up the Keweenaw Peninsula, with Rusty running only thirty-five dollars short.

"Look, I'm going to build a house with that school building. I'm going to pay taxes on it. Don't let it be destroyed!" He sold the school superintendent on the idea.

Rusty rushed off to the secretary of the board of education. "Don't send the wrecker the bill. I'm going to get that building."

Finally, Rusty matched the bid, and the building was theirs.

They needed construction supplies. The same oil distributor who had helped Rusty with the gas station allowed Rusty to use his account, insisting that he always sign the Hellman name for supplies. About a year later, the distributor showed up with a shoe box stuffed full of receipts. Totaled up, they came to eight hundred fifty-four dollars. He also asked for six percent interest. "I told him that seemed awfully high. But he reminded me that I had his money for a long time."

Edith never liked owing bills. By the next year, the house was clear. "We didn't spend extra money for anything," Edith recalls. "Rusty wasn't even allowed to buy a Sunday paper."

They had invested eight hundred fifty-four dollars in the home, "the rest was sweat and barter." It is still their home, a two-story unpretentious house on Main Street where their three children had their own bedrooms, with space for growing and loving in a close family atmosphere.

"I know other politicians try to have the biggest houses in town, but we always felt it was important to be like everybody else, to be like the voters, like the people next door."

Even now, when Edith buys a new car, it is the same shade of green from years past; her winter coat is always the same unpretentious color.

"Folks in the U.P. are no more than two generations away from being a lumberjack or miner. My dad was both. Edith is from a farm family. Up here, we don't have to impress anybody," Rusty says.

Ten terms as township supervisor, and he was learning to control his stutter. Edith's support also gave him confidence. Despite the impediment, despite memory of his seventh grade teacher and the high school principal who had said he would never be able to hold a job that required writing or talking, Rusty started looking at the expanding political arena. With Edith's continuing help, he felt confident that he could completely overcome the speech impediment if he had to. He looked to a seat in the legislature.

But Edith dug in her heels. "No, Daddy. You're not leaving home. The kids are too small, and I'm raising them alone."

It was 1960 and the youngest of their three children was eleven years old when Edith finally consented to his running for representative of the 110th district, a Democrat representing eighty-seven thousand people in the counties of Keweenaw, Houghton, Ontonagon, Gogebic and Iron.

Hating politics all the way, Edith still ran beside him. "He won. I had made myself a widow. I used to get so mad at that damn politics; birthdays, graduations, confirmations, funerals, everywhere I was a widow. He would rush back to Lansing because his secretary was getting married or a buddy had died and he had to be a pallbearer, and again at home I was a widow."

He laughs and she fumes again. "Why do you always laugh when I get mad?"

"Because I know you don't mean it. If you hate politics so much, why are you always climbing on your soapbox?"

And climb she did. Edith traveled the district, a natural speaker at dedications and political rallies, making appointments for Rusty, shoveling dirt at ground breakings.

"She was a real jewel. Many people thought she was the politician."

Edith was his unpaid secretary, his appointment-maker, his chancellor of the exchequer. "He never signed his checks. I could write just like him. If it was an important check, I would sit down and get real nervous and jumpy, growling and shaking and jerking around, and my signature would look just like his. Then I would settle down and become Edith again."

One weekend Rusty walked into his local bank to cash an expense check. The teller asked for identification, and finally called over the bank president.

"Are you having a problem, Rusty?" he asked.

The teller was aghast. "I thought Representative Hellman was a woman," she said.

To friends, Rusty tried to explain that the teller was new in town.

"She's a local lady," Edith objected. "We studied painting together. She knows me well."

In Lansing, Rusty learned "where the boys room and the governor's office are." He prepared himself for his "maiden speech" on the House floor. "That's always the biggie where everyone is scared to death, and mine was a tough one."

The legislature was three weeks into session when a resolution was introduced to assess property values. Rusty felt that the resolution would cut his own house taxes, but from his years as township supervisor, he knew it would also cut tax revenues from the mining companies in half and bring hurt to more people and projects than it could help.

The sponsor of the resolution invited the young legislator to dinner, and proposed that he support his bill. "He intimidated and scared me. I agreed."

However, the more he studied the bill, the more he was convinced that he should vote against it. The sponsor would not compromise.

"You gave your word," he said.

On the House floor, the junior legislator from the U.P. rose to speak.

" 'I rise to oppose this resolution,' " he said, remembering. "Then I told my story. I said I was voting aye to keep my word, but I wanted everyone else to vote nay. When I sat down, I was wringing, sopping wet."

The resolution failed, with only three aye votes.

Politics was contagious. Rusty says once feet get wet in political waters, they never dry out. Edith says embalming fluid is the only cure. He enjoys explaining the philosophy of politics.

"When there were only two people on the face of the earth, it wasn't too hard to get along. When world population expanded to thousands, there were problems. The man with the brain and the muscle wanted all the women and all the meat. The little guy didn't have a chance." It was time for a convention and rules. "Then everybody was entitled to so much meat, and everybody was entitled to a woman or a man and there wasn't so much worry that your neighbor was going to beat you up or bash you over the head for either one."

Rusty says the plan worked for a while until there were millions of people when it grew impossible for everyone to stand up and be heard at these conventions. "So each area elected their own person to go to this big pow-wow and represent their needs, to speak for their decisions. And this person must do everything he possibly can to speak for his people, remembering that to the guy back home, the biggest concern is the road that is running past his own front door.

"This is old-fashioned rural politics, and I felt I had to practice this kind of politics. I felt that I had to give all kinds of services over and above legislative services. Even if it was just a phone call made for a voter, it would have cost him five dollars from up there, so I tried to do it for him down in Lansing."

At the beginning of his second term, Rusty asked to be named to the powerful House Appropriations Committee. "No," came the answer, but he would be named to lesser committees. He refused, saying he would "stay freelance so I can raise hell anywhere I want." He got the Appropriations Committee appointment.

The U.P. boys grew stronger, voting as a body across party lines. Their voting was hard to predict. Legislators would often state that if they knew how the U.P. boys were leaning, they would know if it was time to call for a vote. With agreement from the others, one would stand and make their intentions known. They often voted as a bloc with Wayne County and Detroit, who in turn would support the U.P. "We cared about all of Michigan. With our natural resources, we needed the industries of Detroit."

In Lansing, when one U.P. legislator was invited to dinner, they had to invite them all "or they were in trouble." A long way from home and committed to time in the capital from Monday to Friday, the boys could either hang out in their rooms, the local bars, or sign up for committee work. They signed up for committees, which helped pass the time, but also led to action and power. They told colleagues to introduce any bill they wanted, "but allow the U.P. boys to amend it first so the U.P. doesn't get hurt."

Before he retired, Rusty was the ranking member of the House Appropriations Committee, chairman of the Sub-Committee on the Department of Natural Resources and Agriculture Budgets, and vice chairman of the Joint House and Senate Capital Outlay Committee. "That's where the clout comes from."

Constituents benefited. Before Rusty represented the district, Michigan Technological University had one building added to the campus over a thirty-year period. Under his leadership, they added a building a year. He championed forestry, natural resources, roads, state parks, tourism, public health, public safety, veterans affairs, agriculture and other issues.

He never felt the urge to serve anywhere except the House. It

100

was where he felt comfortable, the best place to serve his constituents. He tells a story that reflects his loyalty.

"I had come home late, very late, and was tired. In the early hours of morning, I was suddenly awakened with Mother poking me over and over. She said, 'Daddy, Daddy, there's a thief in the house, there's a thief in the house.'"

"I rolled over and said, 'Go back to sleep. A thief in the Senate maybe, but never in the House!'"

And he laughed, white head bobbing, wide grin creasing his cheeks.

Legislators from north of the Mackinaw Bridge made the five hundred-mile trip together, bumming rides from the state police, the Department of Natural Resources, flying in and out, pooling rides. Joe Mack started out driving from Ironwood and met Rusty in the village of Covington. At Negaunee, they picked up Jacobetti, dropped south to Escanaba for another, followed U.S. 2 to the bridge and then to Lansing. Along the way, they discussed politics. Rusty boasts that in his twenty-year stint in Lansing, he missed coming home only thirteen weekends.

He recalls one cold winter trip along Lake Michigan when the storm was so bad that the legislators took turns walking with a hand on the front of the car, dragging a foot along the edge of the highway so they could be sure they were still on the road.

"On another trip, temperature was twenty below zero. The northern lights were so beautiful that we stopped the car and got out to watch. The lights were dancing red and yellow and green, hissing across the sky in a spectacular display like you wouldn't believe."

At home in his district, larger in area than the states of Rhode Island, Connecticut, and New Jersey, waited appearances at church bazaars, ball games, fund-raisers, graduations, weddings, parties, Democratic picnics, tournaments, funerals, every parade, "hours upon hours upon hours of visiting with the people. They wanted to see you everywhere: church, the bar, bank, restaurants." Often tieless but seldom without his copper trademark tie tack of a large Upper Peninsula with a tiny mitten of lower Michigan dangling from the Mackinac Bridge, he put Michigan in perspective for the voters.

Edith said once in a while Rusty turned on her, authoritative and bossy. She brought him down fast. "You be careful," she would say. "There are kids voting that were born after you went to Lansing. If you get smart, I'm not going to tell you who they are."

Once Rusty got wind of an occasion being planned by the local Rotary Club. Once a year, the club invited dignitaries.

"They would try and embarrass the hell out of a guest by announcing that he would perform, something like playing the piano – Mozart or Beethoven or whatever he couldn't do. When they invited me, I got wind that they were going to ask me to play the spoons."

With six months notice, Rusty picked up a pair of spoons and learned to play on the House floor in Lansing. Every bill and every debate was done to the accompaniment of the click, click rhythm of the spoons slapping from the palm of Rusty's hand to his leg.

"My leg got sore where I slapped the spoons. I tried to be soft," he says with an impish grin. "The girls up front at the speaker's desk asked me to please learn in a hurry, and even asked Edith if she could get me to stop."

Rusty made his debut, but he hasn't stopped yet. At Lansing's Red Fox Restaurant where all the legislators hang out, he showed up on Wednesday nights with the band.

"They had good-sounding spoons," Rusty says.

Afterward, he would absentmindedly stick them in his pocket, and "first thing I'd know, I'd have a stack in my room and would have to send them back by the handful."

At times, the twenty-year veteran says he retired because he was getting crotchety. But on a more serious note, he talks about legislative powers and the voter in the next county whose primary concern is still the road in front of his house "while I was worried about a five hundred thousand-dollar state budget item. That's too much power. I wasn't representing the people any more."

He is still mounting soapboxes when the need arises, still knocking on Lansing doors, not as a lobbyist, but roaring and prodding in the background making sure things move smoothly for the folks back home.

"I scream and holler and everybody complains about the way I operate, but they know I'm operating," he says with a wide grin.

104

14

AAKVIK

HILMER AAKVIK SAILED away to eternity in his keel-bottomed cedar coffin with the compass carved on top and sturdy marine rope handles for his pallbearers to lift him on his way. It was a fitting departure for a Minnesota North Shore fisherman who knew Lake Superior's temperamental waters about as well as any person.

"Lake Superior is bad enough," he told me a few months before he died in January 1987. "I been in awful storms, but once a fisherman, always a fisherman."

I heard about the fisherman and his knowledge of Superior, as well as the boatlike coffin, in Grand Marais. Villagers in the coffee shop advised me not to go looking for him. "He is old and tired," they said.

Yet as I drove north along the shore road toward the community of Hovland, I found myself searching for the oldest mailbox along the highway. Once I found it, rusting and bent, something compelled me to take the steep, narrow lane leading to the lake. The house was a fisherman's house, worn and tired like the woman in black dress who opened the door to my knock, like the man hunched among deep sagging cushions of the big square chair in front of the television.

But his hands were strong, unwrinkled, steady hands of the fisherman, and his eyes were as blue as the waters he had sailed.

"I still got commercial license but I don't use it this year. Cost me ninety dollars," he said in a heavy accent that betrayed his Norwegian heritage.

He remembered the sunshine of his strength, days of good fish and good sail. But most of all, in the twilight of his years, Hilmer recalled the waters, which year after year tested his soul almost to the limit.

"Worst day on Lake Superior was a calm Sunday morning the latest part of June," he said. "It was so calm was just a ripple. Dem cisco fish happened to be quite a ways out. And here, whole sky got black you would think was end of de world.

"I pay attention to change. It's a good attention. Then it started raining. Raining, lightning and thundering, and there was no time. I was in scow. I had knee boots on, and before I could start motor, my boots fill up. Raining curtains. Fog like pea soup. No compass. I took my bearings from ripples. I hit right the bay, but I can't take any credit. That was pure luck.

"I hit right where I wanted to go. But here was the danger: if I not hit right the bay, if I be going out in the lake in that fog, I was soak wet already and I would have been dead man."

Hilmer folded and unfolded his huge hands and slowly turned to gaze over his shoulder at the inland sea.

"I haven't fished it always," he said. "When I was fourteen and half years old, I was sent from my island in Norway to the Bering Sea. I fished the North Sea, Atlantic, Pacific. And then I fished Lake Superior for more than sixty years.

"Lake Superior is bad enough," he repeated.

Leaning forward, I asked the fisherman about the Carnegie medal I heard mentioned in the town. He ran a hand against his jutting chin and nodded his white head, remembering.

"Thirty years ago," he said. "Neighbor boy Carl Hammer. About twenty-four–twenty-five years old. Was in navy on destroyer. Came home to fish. I warned him time and again. That was prophetic. Life on destroyer different than skiff on Lake Superior.

"We fished together out there. He was awfully careless with his gasoline. Two times before he had close call. He went out again and it was too late.

"November, one-two days before Thanksgiving when weather starting to be serious. But steelhead were running. He was going to set two nets, then the storm came. Had only rubberized canvas gloves, didn't have woolen choppers like I had. And he depended on the motor. Then he was a mile and a half out and it was too late.

"Flat-bottom skiff drifts like a chip. Well, I suppose if he had of hold onto the nets he would have been all right. Or if he had let out his two dry nets, he wouldn't have drifted so far. Was come a gale when we knew he was missing.

"I prepared to come out. Was six above zero. Lake started steaming worse than fog, thirty-forty feet up in the air. Couldn't see nothin', but with my experience and sixteen-foot flat-bottom skiff, I thought I could find him.

"Out there, my motor stopped. I monkeyed with it and saw was no use. I laid it on bottom of skiff. Waves picking up seven-eight feet. Skiff was quarter full of water and I had to get it out. I was prepared. Bailed water. Had one reliable Johnson motor extra. In order to get water out of skiff I had to throw bad one overboard.

"Seas were building something fierce. I had fish box and manila rope. Dat fish box weigh fifty pounds. I tied rope onto fish box and threw overboard as sea anchor.

"By then I was forty-fifty miles out and waves build up twenty–twenty-three feet high. It was pretty near dark then. Everything froze from the spray and I was chopping ice. I was busy man!

"Coast Guard chopper come over, pretty near took the cap off me, and I never saw him again. A two hundred-foot Coast Guard cutter was out. He laid in at Chicago Bay that night and I could see the lights but I can't get to him. I would like to see dat skipper and I would tell him somethin'.

"I got the motor started again. All night I chip ice. The spray was continual. I didn't even have time to pray, but I didn't expect an angel to come and pick me up to take me shore anyway.

"I was on the lake twenty-nine hours. Wind had changed to the west-northwest. Skiff was leaking. No spray then, had let up. Out of gas. Only means of salvation was to row. My woolen choppers froze. I yust thinking about my brand-new all-wool flannel shirt. Should I cut up my new shirt and make strips for hands? Den I thought, 'No use.' Skiff leaking anyway. And I looked up to see Coast Guard boat.

"I was mile and half from shore. I would have made it to shore on my own power.

"After dat, we had two weeks offshore wind and we never found missing boat. I think when Carl had nothing to chop ice and all that spray, he fixed up top half of his skiff and it got top-heavy. In heavy seas boat would turn sideways. I figure that would have been around nine–ten o'clock night he got lost."

Hilmer did not mention the Carnegie medal for heroism, which he was awarded for his rescue efforts. Instead, he said he had fished Lake Superior during the "Great Depression when couldn't sell anything. Had team of horses. Had box to take fish in. Got six cents a pound, but I was lucky. I had cisco rig and that was only thing would sell. I lived all right, you see."

And he was ready to die, meeting the approaching sunset with a chuckle.

"Hereafter nothing to worry about," he said with a twinkle in his eyes. "I got my boat for trip. Tried it on for size. Ready for calm seas ahead. I give sixty dollars to build fine coffin but the carpenter hardly didn't want to take it.

"I've seen quite a bit in my lifetime. I'll be ninety in three weeks. It's about time to go aloft, like the old sailors say. . . . "

And he did.

15

HORIZON

H IGH ABOVE ONTARIO'S LAKES and boulder-filled rivers, a bush pilot banks his small floatplane to watch fog rolling inland from Lake Superior. Slowly, soundlessly, surreptitiously, silvery fog creeps across peaks and valleys, hovering to envelop forests and scattered roads.

The pilot turns northward away from the gathering fog and toward a remote camp accessible only by floatplane. "For most people, it's the romance of getting there that counts," says Don Massey.

The big man with eyes on the horizon heads Air-Dale Flying Service at Hawk Junction northeast of Wawa. He flies fishermen, hunters and other outdoor enthusiasts into bush country, like mercy flights from civilization, rescues from ringing phones, five o'clock traffic, meetings and deadlines. He leaves them at outpost camps, pilgrims on sabbatical with nature until prearranged pickup time inevitably rolls around.

Massey heads for a blue lake surrounded by tall forests. On a spit of peninsula stands a log cabin, nestled so close in the trees that only the telltale smoke of the breakfast fire signals its location. He says the romance of getting there is a main factor in the bush experience. It stamps ownership on lakes and forests and a self-imposed isolation with friends and nature, a dream that no one should hold license to casually invade.

Massey studies the landscape and frowns, eyes squinting, brow furrowed in concern. Below, a new road cuts through the forest toward his destination lake. One more road into an area once accessible only by air, one more threat to the bush experience, to a life-style that Massey says is disappearing. Too fast.

"For the bush pilot, there are no more good lakes to discover and no places left to expand," he says with a faraway look in his eyes.

Every year, he sees remoteness carved from the bush as more logging roads reach long arms closer to wilderness camps. Massey says there are efforts to restrict these roads to forestry use, but "it's not that easy." Four-wheel vehicles climb or circumvent barriers to appear uninvited at isolated lakes and cabins.

While the romance of north country lingers, Massey wakes every morning to the beckoning skies, following a way of life that began as a childhood dream as subtle as the fog of Lake Superior. It began at his parents' tourist camp in southern Ontario. "One of the guys who lived down the lake would bring his plane up. I'd stand and watch him fly in and settle on the lake. I got the bug and never lost it," he recalls.

Massey learned to fly in 1965 at Toronto. Somehow, city bustle with the rush of people didn't fit with the freedom he found in the skies. He drove north to Lake Superior country, and "I'm still here." He based his flying service in Wawa, contending with restless fog, which would rush over the mountains from Superior to envelop the town.

"It could be sunshine at the airport, and five miles away, you couldn't see across the street," he said. "I spent fifteen years in Wawa looking at the fog. That was long enough."

Massey moved his operation north to Hawk Junction. With his pilots, he operates within a seventy-mile radius, flying

Beaver and Otter floatplanes, which he says are designed for Ontario's small lakes. Air-Dale flies parties of fishermen and hunters to remote cabin locations. Along with their outdoor gear are piles of sleeping bags and personal items, boxes of coffee, pancake flour, eggs, beans, steaks, cookies, and other food items. Cooking utensils aren't necessary. They're on the cabin shelves.

"Most of the parties bring in too much. They only need a change of clothing. This is the bush!"

When Massey returns to pick them up, most boast of big catches of fish or quotas of game. Moose are quartered for easier transport. Loading up the gear, Massey keeps a watchful eye on float load lines and weight control.

"There are not many daredevil bush pilots anymore. We try hard not to break up our planes," he said.

Pilots are harder to come by, especially with escalating insurance rates and the lure of higher pay in the cities. "It's not so much flying the small planes as the hard work and long hours," he said. "And the hardest part is that it's a six-months-a-year job."

Massey finds no pleasure in winter flying. He had rather contend with summer fog than winter's heavy snow and slush. "In winter, I can take off for a half-hour flight, and be gone three hours trying to dig my plane out of the snow to fly back home again."

Yet for Massey, the bush is the only place to live, and life to this pilot is flying. Massey compares himself to a "big glorified taxi driver," but he wouldn't change jobs with anyone. "It's the only kind of real flying there is anymore."

He would never trade his seat in the floatplane for the controls of a jet. "Jet pilots had sooner be doing this, too, except the money ain't so good. Every trip, I see something different."

Flying low to take in the landscape, Massey spots a campfire, a tent, moose browsing among lily pads of a shallow lake. He watches for hikers who might be lost. Dipping a wing, he comes down for a closer look at an overturned canoe floating down a swollen river, hoping he won't spot someone floating beside it, praying they've affected their own rescue. Seeing nothing, he calls on his radio and flies on.

South of Hawk Junction, he watches for the treacherous fog that can sweep off Superior like an icy gray ghost, but finds only sunshine.

"You gotta keep a good healthy respect for the big lake and not play around with it," he says. "At times I have taxied out and fog has rolled in by the time I bank. Fog has trapped a lot of people who can't believe it can form that fast."

For Massey, unpredictable weather is part of the job. And he finds an advantage in the floats he flies: floats can land anywhere. He says it's the guys on wheels who get in trouble when fog rolls in and they're caught without enough fuel to make the next landing site. "I don't land on Lake Superior too often, but there are always inland lakes."

Studying the skies again, he continues, "I have seen the weather change in minutes. I love it, but there are probably more airplanes that have gone missing along Lake Superior than anywhere in the country."

He tells of helicopter rescues off a rugged beach after pilots became disoriented in fog and went down, and other pilots even less fortunate who hit the mountains or simply disappeared.

"Somebody has been doing this kind of flying since the invention of airplanes," he says. He's glad he is still part of this select breed.

He talked on, about Superior, fog, silence of the forests, remote inland lakes, smoke rising from a lone camper's fire, fish at evening and moose at dawn – the bush.

"I'm not ready to lose it," he says wistfully.

16

MICHIGAN SLIM

"I'VE GOT RIP VAN Winkle beat all to heck," said Max Hackel, a self-imposed but sociable hermit, who spent the best part of fifty years living alone on the jack pine plains of Michigan's Upper Peninsula.

The tall, angular trapper was known as Michigan Slim. Toward the latter part of his life, he ambled through the door of his rustic cabin and watched the sun duck behind the jack pine forest bordering his Grasshopper Ranch.

Settling on a convenient log, he reflected on fishing and the outdoors he had found more tantalizing than the job and wife he had left behind, and the solitude of the woods where deer and whiskey jacks, or Canada jays, call more regularly than friends.

"Love for the woods ruined most of my life," he said. "Well, not ruined. But I didn't cut much of a swath, either."

In 1934, Slim pulled up alongside the blacksmith shop of a deserted lumber camp on the sand plains west of Big Bay. He shoved open the door and threw aside scattered bits of rusted logging tools. He shooed away a few porcupines, cleared a corner for his bed, and moved in.

Slim never wandered too far from his camp after that eventful day. He removed the rest of the porcupine litter, hauled in wood for the big round barrel stove, and settled in. Years slipped past as Slim trapped and fished, and did a little guiding, gambling, reading and sitting. He was not in a hurry because there was no place he wanted to go. Slim became the master of his days where the sun rose gently, twilight crept through the woods on tiptoe and night silence settled easily into dreams. He watched spring melt away the snow and coax open the eyes of the violets. He watched while summer set the trout to leaping near the waterfalls on the streams and fall roll blazing reds and golds across the forest.

During his later years when he was well past eighty, Slim moved into the village for the winter months, his one concession to the inconveniences of time. From his two-room winter cabin on the outskirts of Big Bay, he made occasional trips into the village to round up a pinochle partner, pick up his mail and scrounge for a book or two. His incessant reading prompted local folks to refer to him as "the educated trapper." "I read everything once, some things twice," he said.

Come spring, he loaded his books, his bright plaid woolen shirts, long underwear, and assortment of hats into his car that ran on faith, and headed back down the rutted road to the "ranch" until winter came again.

Life had not always been so orderly for Slim. Young Max Hackel had married the daughter of a blacksmith in Flint. In 1918, he joined the army, and spent most of his tour in England and France. There had been a few quick trips to Spain, in later years provoking old memories strong enough to restore a twinkle in his eye and a smile across his face.

"Despite the threat of being thrown into the hoosegow, we let ourselves be lured across the Basque Mountains by those beautiful senoritas," he recalled.

He returned home in 1919 with a couple of thousand dollars won off the blankets rolling dice, and discovered that his wife had run off with a stonemason.

Slim took a drag from his crooked hand-rolled cigarette and recalled gambling throughout the Midwest and Canada. "Sometimes I had a wad–sometimes I didn't." He grimaced at the memory of the counterfeiter who slipped him a handful of bad bills during a crap game over the old A & P store in Marquette. "I had to go all the way to Sault Ste. Marie and federal court to straighten that one out."

Wide-open gambling spots such as the ones along Minnesota's Mesabi Range lured him to hit half a dozen games a weekend. Although he ran a regular circuit, he claimed it was "just to make a few ten spots to go fishing." However, legends claim that during Prohibition his moonshining operations also helped fatten his fishing bankroll. Not that he needed much of a bankroll. He was a worm fisherman, disdaining the citified fisherman who fished his streams with flies. "There's not a bit of nourishment in them," he complained.

A swing from Lower Michigan through the Upper Peninsula in 1925 changed his life-style for a while. He took a stroll through the forests and decided to stay. And the gambler gambled on matrimony once again. He married a music teacher from Munising, landed a job with an oil company, and tried domestication.

Slim worked hard. He tried to show up for work on time and put in his mandatory day. But then trout season would interfere, and bird season, and other seasons best enjoyed outdoors. And how could a person be expected to deliver oil during deer season?

In those days, some school boards frowned on employing married schoolmarms, so his wife lost her job. Depression times squeezed harder, and Slim checked out. "I couldn't keep up with the way she was used to living, so we split up," he said.

The tall, lanky woodsman headed up the curving road north of Marquette toward Big Bay. He turned off short of the village and headed into the dusty jack pine plains. In a quiet hollow at the end of an old railroad spur that once served the lumber camps that harvested tall virgin pines, Slim found the one-room blacksmith shop.

Some of the old logging camps were still in operation. He

occasionally signed on with them for a few weeks, or took temporary work with a road construction crew, but never long enough to let work interfere seriously with trapping and fishing.

With his extra bankroll, he added a room or lean-to to his homestead. He cut spruce and balsam logs from a nearby swamp, shouldered the smaller ones to the ranch, and dragged the big ones. He squared the kitchen walls with a taut fishing line and stacked the timbers shoulder high. He tacked on a precariously slanted tar paper roof and added a window here and there. Had he known the bears would claim the windows for a runway, he might have made them smaller. Lastly, Slim added a woodshed, including an indoor-outdoor two-holer in the corner.

Into the kitchen he moved an imposing wood-burning wrought iron kitchen range and chairs of questionable stability, adding orange crate shelves for cans of soup and fruit, reserving a space for a few plates, bowls and cups. However, except for a cup for the coffee that was always brewing on the stove, he had little need for the plates or bowls. Somehow, soup or stew from an empty number three peaches can always tasted better.

In his other room with the hand-hewn bed, Slim dragged a well-worn horsehair sofa closer to his big round barrel heater where he could curl his long legs toward the fire on cold winter days and read.

Surveying his handiwork, he named it Grasshopper Ranch. "Won't grow anything but grasshoppers in this sand," he said.

Slim had no need to seek outside adventure, for adventure came to Slim. Summer seared the sand prickly hot; winter sometimes piled snow that reached the slanting rooftop. In 1939, one such storm howled on for days. With coffee perking on the stove, plenty of wood in the box and books to read, Slim was content. Then one morning he awakened in darkness, with drifts piled against the windows. Slim opened the heater door and kindled the last of the evening coals. The pipe was choked with snow! Heat and breakfast coffee could be forgotten. Slim was buried in the drifts.

Tugging at the front door, Slim opened it to a solid world of white. He grabbed a snowshoe and started digging. "I burrowed a hole in the bank with the heel of the snowshoe, heaved my backpack outside, then crawled out myself."

The hermit trudged through the drifts and biting wind toward the nearest lumber camp. His eyelashes froze; an icicle slowly formed, dangling from the end of his nose. "I don't know how cold it was, but I had an awfully cold smile when I made it into camp."

Once the storm let up, the camp boss hired Slim at fifty cents an hour (top price, he recalled) to help clear the Hungry Hollow Road and back to the Grasshopper Ranch.

Although it was not by invitation or to his pleasure, Slim shared his ranch with the local bears. He tolerated their foraging as long as they showed proper respect, for killing them would have required a burial detail. Being a hermit, burying meant work and work meant Slim.

One day while Slim was off checking out the Salmon Trout River, another bear came calling. After taking his usual peek through the kitchen window and noticing no one around, old Mr. Bear gave the window a hearty shove. Once the glass was shattered, he pushed and pulled himself inside. And once inside, he helped himself. Slim found the overturned molasses bucket in the middle of the floor, with sticky footprints marching across the floor and out through another broken window.

However, the bear that helped himself to Slim's swill bucket stretched hospitality too far. Slim was returning from another peaceful day on the Salmon Trout River with a creel full of fish when the bear surprised Slim about the same time Slim surprised the bear. The bear had been head-deep in the swill bucket, searching for a delicacy.

"I had a chew in my mouth," Slim said. "When he looked up, I spit in his face. He took off in a hurry."

However, the bear returned again to his newly found banquet. As determined as the bear was to dine, Slim was just as determined to save his bucket. To lose it would mean a trip to the village to buy another, along with a lost day of fishing. Finally, Slim tied the bucket to a grindstone and wired it tight.

One twilight, Slim was standing contentedly at the cookstove stirring mulligan stew when a rare visitor came to call. Through the patched window, he saw his seven-foot Swedish friend Gus Dahl round the woodshed. Gus, along with Slim, was among a rare collection of bachelors who had taken up residences in the abandoned logging camps around Big Bay. The new growth of jack pines were scattered with characters such as Gus, Slim, and Tin Can Sullivan, who got his name from his habit of eating from tin cans, then throwing them onto the pile at his cabin door.

As Gus approached Slim's door that evening, Slim saw that it was already too late to warn him when he caught his glimpse of the bear at the bucket. The bear had already spotted Gus. He charged at full speed, knocking Gus flat. The big Swede hit the ground on a roll and rolled right back on his feet again, with legs churning. His running record was as good as ever. Like Slim, he had outrun matrimony and outrun work. Now Gus outran the bear. He made it all the way to the kitchen with giant steps befitting his imposing height. "I killed that one the next night. Or a dead ringer for him. I didn't ask him his name," chuckled Slim.

But the burial posed the expected problems, and more. Slim's sand plains form only a thin coating with underlying, unyielding, glaciated rock. Slim loaded the bear onto the back of his truck and headed along a section of road toward Big Bay where he thought the sand would be deeper. Digging down several feet, he dumped the bruin in on his back, stuffed in four legs and piled on the sand. Slim drove on to town for his mail and the week's groceries, visited friends and paid a few bills. On the way home, he slowed the car as he approached the new grave. Then something along the sandy bank caught his eye. Curious, he pulled over to watch.

Ever so slowly, the mound of sand began to shift and quiver. First a set of claws rose slowly from the sand, then another and another and another until four big paws appeared. They were followed by four furry legs, stiffening as they came. Slim hadn't allowed for rigor mortis!

"I had to bury that bear again. After that, I didn't shoot unless they put up too much of an argument," said Slim. "I don't even shoot porcupines. They prowl around here thicker than chipmunks, and don't have brains enough to be scared. But it's easier to chase them with a stick than bury them."

Folks decided that Slim kept the matters of wildlife so peaceful around the ranch that they appointed him justice of the peace, a position he filled in Michigan Slim-style for twelve years. He even performed a wedding once.

The couple knocked on the door to announce their intentions. They brushed through woolen socks, long johns and an assortment of shirts steaming over the drum heater. In the kitchen they found cans of peaches and stacks of cereal boxes covering almost every inch of the table, except for the space reserved for the beaver that Slim was busy skinning. Slim slid the beaver onto a crate near the stove while he performed the ceremony. Later, he said he may as well have left the beaver stretched fresh on the table, with no attempts to tidy up. The marriage didn't last, anyway.

Before he died on the shy side of ninety, Slim looked back over the years spent with deer and bear and other wildlife roaming across his yard of wild timothy and clover. He recalled the tumbling, twisting Salmon Trout River with fish below the rapids and white birch along the banks.

"There's not much romance in the life of a fisherman and trapper living alone," he said. "Unless you like quiet sunsets, trout tugging at your line and the sound of partridge drumming in the hardwood."

17

HOME OF THE GOLDEN-BREASTED WOODPECKER

SOME PEOPLE ARE born to an island way of life. Others happen upon it later and never want to leave, gauging their lives by ferries that move back and forth the two and one-half miles across the North Channel of Chequamegon Bay between Madeline Island and Bayfield, Wisconsin; gauging their lives by seasons with open waters and winters when the bay freezes and the air boats take over the ferry runs; gauging their lives with antiquity and ancestors who can be traced not by documented family trees but by a slight depression in the forest floor or a younger stand of trees or sometimes only a memory lingering in the corners of the mind of the very old. Sometimes the island and native way of life is left to others such as Nori Newago to gently prod her own young blonde native Americans into the historic past carved by their ancestors, not only of their blonde

123

roots inherited from a blonde mother, but from the native American heritage of their father.

Nori fell in love with Joe Newago, a Madeline Islander and member of the Ojibwa Nation, after he returned from the armed services and walked across the ice to Bayfield where she was working. She never again wanted to live away from the island and the lake. Most mornings, Nori and husband Joe are out of bed early to watch the sun rising over Chequamegon Bay.

"Joe sits there," she says, pointing to the chair across the breakfast table. "I sit here, and we focus on the lake."

Through the picture window, they look across a beach of sand with a large uprooted tree and water stretching blue off to the east. On the horizon, a big ball of sun peeks over Superior, rising slowly in a changing rainbow of purple and pink. Then it leaps into view full-born, pink changing to a brilliant red pendant to dangle above the water like fire on a string. They watch the colors on the water, deep green, turquoise, light blue with green undertones, and Joe measures the depths by the shades.

Nori and Joe feel the power in the water "like it has a life and pattern of its own." Sometimes glassy calm, sometimes violent and thrashing and roaring.

Every morning of all the seasons brings its surprises, Nori said. "In spring, we can see the shore of Michigan misty on the horizon. A blue heron flies past on its way to the open bay, an eagle soars overhead. In the fall after a storm with the wind coming up at night, we wake to see an ore boat or two anchored in the bay. Winter mornings, ice is in, ice is out, ice piling up on the beach. Maybe a coyote runs across the ice."

Madeline Island sits like an afterthought offshore from Bayfield, Wisconsin, gateway to the Apostle Islands. Madeline is the only one of the twenty-two Apostles outside the Apostle Islands National Lakeshore. There are forty-five miles of roads, mostly unpaved, a state park, and a mixture of homes varying from log cabins to weathered clapboard, modern condos of the summer people, and the Newagos' own neat cottage on the bay. For about one hundred fifty permanent residents including fifty members of the Ojibwa Nation, there is no place like it on earth.

The island, first called Moningwunakauning, or "Island of the Golden-Breasted Woodpecker," was renamed at the wedding of Ojibwa Chief White Crane's daughter Equaysayway to Michel Cadotte, factor for the North West company. As a wedding gift, White Crane gave his daughter the Christian name Madeline. He also bestowed the name upon the island.

Nori understands when some outsiders see the negative side of island life. It is not for everyone, with the ferries, single grocery store, a few restaurants, one bar open during the winter months, one year-round church and a two-room schoolhouse. "If the ferry and island-living bothers you, there is no sense in being here."

For islanders, the summer ferry is a fifteen-minute break, a visiting time, an organizing time, wind-down time and a time for making grocery lists. Come winter, then spring and melting of the winter road which curves in and out of the Christmas trees, islanders must force themselves to rethink the ferry schedule for every trip to the mainland.

For Nori, understanding of island ways, of Joe and other native Americans, came through knowing his mother. "She didn't question or try to change. There was this quiet acceptance of the island, of nature and everything around her."

Nori never feared for Joe when he is fishing the big lake; he grew up with waves and ice. He knows its moods and temperament. Each winter, Joe is one of the first men on the island to walk across with a chisel to test thickness of the ice. "He doesn't trust anyone else to do it."

When the ice is strong and solid, Joe and other villagers take to snowmobiles, wind sleds, or trucks to plant Christmas trees to mark a safe route for the winter road from the island to the mainland.

After a busy summer when tourists swell the island population to more than three thousand, winter is a time of getting to know one another again, of touching base, community potluck dinners, crafts in the community center with babies underfoot and husbands stopping in for lunch.

It is in this caring village that Nori raised her four children. She watched them grow healthy and strong like their father, roaming the beaches of singing sand, roaming rich forests of oak, maple, birch and aspen with a scattering of spruce; searching for agates; climbing sandstone ledges; exploring shoreline caves; leaping across the wetlands from one grassy clump to another.

They walked through the Old Mission Cemetery, which is now on private land, and the more recent Indian cemetery near the marina, studying grave houses and gravestones where Ojibwas lie still and silent beside French and British explorers, soldiers and voyageurs. Their father recalled Old Mission Church with cedar and birch bark lining interior walls and ceilings. Ojibwa relatives told about the burial houses, which they explained were a product of Christianity. To Ojibwas, the whole island was a burial ground, with the dead buried near the camps where elders and chiefs allowed grasses and forests to grow and the ground to return to nature, growing wild, letting the lake claim its own, letting the spirits go.

Listening, Nori learned, feeling as though she was almost an islander, too. "I learned that anyone can walk with nature," she said.

She watched as young Steve, her son, learned to call in loons, call down an owl, coax a squirrel almost to his out-stretched hand, talk to the deer, to hunt but not to waste a shot or food.

Islanders passed on their history, stories of children going to school in a buggy warmed by a kerosene stove, of winter mail by dogsled, and later, Joe's mother baking lugelait, a soda bread, with about a dozen kids clamoring for the crusty heel.

Nori learned the ways of modern islanders: self-sufficiency and making-do; heading for the opposite shore and the doctor with the first childbirth pains; getting children off to the two-room and one-teacher school through the eighth grade, then sending them on the ferry or winter airboat to catch the school bus waiting on the docks in Bayfield. She reminded her children to take a toothbrush along to school for the nights they need to stay over because of bad weather or a sports event or other activity.

"There is always a schoolmate or pal to take them in. Or we have an understanding with other parents." Nori says these arrangements work well; mainland children in turn always have a summer home on the island with their friends.

She watched islanders, and joined them in sending her children to whichever of the two churches were conducting services. "St. John's United Church of Christ has been here since 1925. St. Joseph's Catholic Church is open summers, with a priest coming over from Bayfield on Saturday evenings. In winter, everybody goes Protestant. We were ecumenical here before it was popular."

Nori learned to understand Joe's need to fish, whether or not he is catching anything. She understands his need to be on the water, drifting, free. But Nori never understood him better than the bad time after she saw smoke lifting from the village.

The Newagos were living in an old farmhouse on a rise of ground above La Pointe when she saw the puff of smoke. "I thought kids in town must be playing with matches," she said. Then a friend pounded on her door and shouted, "Grab your purse."

"I knew it was Joe and I would be leaving the island."

There had been an explosion, and Joe was badly burned. He was hospitalized for a month, but confinement was worse than the pain. He begged to go home to the island, begged for a way of escape. When all else failed, he would step outside his room onto the fire escape, searching for space and open sky, gazing over the expanse of distant lake, searching for the horizon, the sunrise, sunset, noonday, midnight.

Nori, too, has learned this need for space. "We cannot be anonymous on the island. There is no 'mad corner' in which to hide. At times like this, on this small island, we can only turn to the lake," she said.

Drive any island road and few houses can be seen; circle the island in a boat and there they are, beachside, where islanders can savor the water and the view.

Like so many young islanders, three of the Newagos' four children have left. They return often, bringing home their own young families to experience their heritage. They joke about

127

trying to swim in "yucky inland waters" after cold, invigorating Lake Superior, about coming home, about the dog whose family moved to the mainland but he found his way to the docks and caught the ferry back to Madeline.

Gone are the legends before the first French explorers came to the island in the mid-1600s. More so than Joe, Nori enjoys stories of fur traders, voyageurs and trading posts, of generations of Cadottes who married Ojibwa women, ancestors of the Newagos and others.

The Ojibwa Nation retains strong ties to Madeline Island, its spiritual home. Nori says there is an awakening of this heritage all along the lakeshore.

Joe feels his heritage in the water and trees, singing sands, spring green of budding trees, the force of nature on the water.

"There is a difference here, a mystique. I can feel it," Nori says.

18

ICE OUT!

WHEN SPRING ICE breaks up in the Black River and surges through the gorge toward the mouth, the year-round residents in the village of Black River Harbor throw heavy mackinaws around their shoulders and rush for the banks.

The Black River narrows for half a mile above the natural harbor mouth at Lake Superior, squeezing through deep gorges and leaping down ledges in a series of waterfalls. In winter, falls hum to near-silence with only a muffled stirring under the tons of river ice. When the arbutus blossom and the sun strikes the western exposures, a stirring of spring is felt in the forest. Chipmunks scurry about. Deer paw at snow-covered mosses along the banks. Residents monitor the thaw on almost a minute-to-minute basis until, like a modern Paul Revere, someone shouts the news.

"Ice out! Ice out!" comes the cry as they rush down the tree-lined village street that parallels the river. And all activity stops. Work. Play. Sleep.

It is the birthing of spring.

Whispering begins high up on the Upper Peninsula's Copper Peak – thawing, melting, shifting, cracking, then the pell-mell rush downstream to surge over Great Conglomerate Falls, through Gorge Falls, Potowatomi, Sandstone and Rainbow. Great bergs and chunks of ice duck under Black River Harbor's suspension bridge, which was built during a winter while workmen could haul supplies over the frozen river. Ice continues its breakup as it bumps into the harbor, grinding along marina pilings and on to Lake Superior.

"Ice out" signals the opening of the harbor for the season and the return of fishermen who have sailed these shores for as long as memories reach. Ojibwas who braved the waters in birchbark canoes, voyageurs paddling their bateaux and finally the charter fishermen of today.

"Ice out" is one of many natural wonders that bring folks time and again to this quaint spot beside the inland sea: spring flowers and squeaky-clean beaches; summer fishing and pleasure boating; autumns so beautiful and forests so brilliant with color that it almost stops the breath, until a windstorm comes and strips the trees of their bright castanet leaves and blows them all away. Then winter returns with its endless cycle of frosty rivers and white magic on the forest until "Ice out," and spring thaw comes again.

The sixteen miles of County Road 513 from Bessemer to Black River Harbor winds through hardwood forests, past abandoned farms and Big Powderhorn Ski Resort, with Indianhead and Blackjack ski slopes just across the hills. From Ironwood, County Road 505 connects with County Road 204 which cuts through blueberry and raspberry meadows and past the farm that for a long time was called "Place Where the Man Shot His Wife." There, the roads converge to swing through deep forests and around Copper Peak, then down a tunnel of trees to the village and the lake. Black River Harbor is the most remote village along Michigan's Lake Superior south shore.

Residents and those who come often to the harbor are drawn by the lake, mesmerized by its waves which tend to purge the mind of cares. Those who stand on shore feel shyly proud to be so near this great body of water, as though standing proud next

to a celebrity. And to brave its cold waters is as refreshing as a kiss at sunrise.

Dean and Peggy Krohn moved to the harbor in 1984 to operate the Bear Track Inn. The Krohns were working in Illinois when they decided to look around for vacation property. Dean had often visited Gogebic County. When he heard the rustic Bear Track cabins were for sale, he bought them. Two weeks later, Peggy moved into the main lodge with their two yellow Labradors, Kelly and Little Bear; Dean continued his truck-driving job until the business could support them both. He commuted on weekends.

"I had never operated a wood-burning stove, and that was my primary heat," Peggy said. "I was petrified that the fire would go out!"

Throughout the winter, Peggy rented the Bear Track cabins to her customers, and moved her belongings and dogs into whichever cabin stood empty for the night. "Villagers called me the harbor hobo," she said.

One night she inadvertently rented all her cabins to skiers from the nearby resorts, forgetting to save one for herself. She faced the night in a storage basement until a neighbor took her in.

A few months later, she and Dean bought the Sail Inn, and became an integral part of village life. Neighbors help in the restaurant on busy nights, waitressing, cooking, or, in the case of John Ramsay, plunking out tunes on the old piano.

Besides the Bear Track and Sail Inn, the village has several summer resorts and an antique shop. Boaters and picnickers frequent the marina and the U.S. Forest Service park and hike the trails to the waterfalls. Some backpackers hike down the North Country Trail, which cuts through the Ottawa National Forest. A few wooden fishing boats of days gone by weather the seasons under gnarled apple trees or clutter behind barns like cast-off cars.

The Chippewa came more than two hundred years ago in an annual pilgrimage over the Indian trail from the warmer Mississippi, through Lac du Flambeau, to small tepee villages on the present site of Bessemer and at the Black River mouth.

Then came white fishermen who built huts along the conglomerate reef across the river, fishermen such as Matt Maki, Abel Eikkinen, Henry Muhonen and others whose first names have been forgotten – Drolson, Clemens. After break-up, they shoved their open fishing boats into the cold water, weathering the shifting of the waves and storms that always came.

At season's end, they pulled their boats from the water on huge rollers and parked them for the winter beside their huts at river's edge. Some went into the forests to cut wood until spring. Others huddled in their huts near their boats.

With spring, activity returned to the lake. At times people from town bartered for a charter, such as the time Muhonen took the priest fishing. Once their boat pulled away from the harbor, the priest started serious fee negotiations. He let it be known that Muhonen had spent many a season away from church. Perhaps the fee should go toward penance.

Muhonen refused to negotiate.

Finally the priest admitted that he had empty pockets – no money! Now it was Muhonen's turn to negotiate.

"You yust leave long black robe mit me," Muhonen said. "When you get money, I gif' back robe."

Muhonen got paid.

Black River Harbor could tell many a tale of the past, if one could decipher the river's murmurings and its roar. However, some have been preserved. There's the tale of Teabones, the World War I draft dodger, who showed up at the harbor with his wife and a passel of kids. They showed up sometime before 1920 and walked off into the rugged Porcupine Mountains, where they lived off the land, Teabones hiking out occasionally for supplies.

One cold winter day, Teabones showed up at the shack of the fisherman Muhonen carrying a small pack on his back. Muhonen invited him in. Teabones eased off the pack to warm his half-frozen hands around a cup of steaming coffee. He retrieved a sandwich from his pack and, munching it, talked about the cold.

Finally he arose to leave. He must be on his way, he said. Their last child, which Teabones had delivered himself, had been stillborn, he said, and his wife insisted on a proper burial. Teabones had placed the babe in the pack, along with a sandwich, and was on his way over the trail to Bessemer and the cemetery.

Some time later, a wagon road was cut to Bessemer. Store owners and fish peddlers made the all-day trip to the harbor to buy fish. As roads improved, it became a popular Sunday afternoon outing for folks from Bessemer, Wakefield and Ironwood. Others sailed over from Bayfield, Wisconsin, and anchored in the harbor. Visitors picnicked beside the river and bought fish and other goods from the cardboard or roughly nailed-together booths they called cantinas. Artists brought along easels and paints, or sketched the old fishing boats beside the growing number of fishing shacks.

The Christianson family moved their fishing operations eastward from Madeline Island. Tom charged ten cents a customer for a ride in his paddleboat across the river to the beaches. Return trip was free.

Tom and his father, Martin, operated their gas-powered

fishing tug, the first in the harbor to be operated without sail and the first of several that the Christiansons either built or helped to build. Along with other fishermen – Victor Leppanen, Doug Allen, Walt Speaker – they pitched in to repair the break wall in an attempt to hold back the sea which annually clogged the mouth with sand to block their access.

Vick Leppanen kept his boat, the *Nancy Jean*, until he died. He was as handy with boats and engines as he was at catching fish. Folks tell of the time he helped Stanley "Stash" Johnson install a Studebaker engine in Johnson's boat, the *Playmate*. On its first trip out, the engine blew the top right off! "Vick called Dad a daredevil for that one," said Tommy Johnson. They cooled the engine, dumped water in the radiator with a handy bucket, and paddled for shore. And they switched to more traditional engines.

Then the fish decline came. Old-timers blame the introduction of coho salmon with their "ravenous appetites, which interrupted the established fish cycle." They also blame new laws for keeping them ashore, turning them to chartering, while fishermen with Indian permits continue to lay their nets.

There are fishermen such as Jimmy Johnson who are thankful for any excuse to sail on Lake Superior. Jimmy runs fishing charters for tourists, yet he mourns with every sunset for the old days when he and his father joined other commercial fishermen in the harbor. He burns with jealousy of other fishermen who still hold the right to commercially cast their lines and nets into the lake he loves.

Johnson says that he never met the fisherman from Wisconsin who most frequently fishes this shore, but he harbors an intense one-way love-hate relationship for the man.

"He is married to an Indian, so he can fish," Johnson says. "I respect him and I love him because he is a good fisherman. But I hate him because the government is letting him participate in things I cannot do.

"I don't care about making money," he says.
The lake is my existence;
The lake is my life;

134

ICE OUT!

The lake is my dream.
I know the lake. . .
It is part of me.
I love the lake as much as he does;
That is why I cry for him.
I cannot fish alongside him.
I cannot compete.
I go out on the deep blue water and
There are his nets
All around me
And I can't fish.

He bows his head. His shoulders sag. Tomorrow there will be another charter, but that is not enough. Jimmy Johnson is a fisherman.

The village has changed along with the lake. The Forest Service took over the park from Gogebic County. They burned the old boats that stood at tipsy angles along the river and the rotting huts of the fishermen. The cantinas never returned.

Vick Leppanen kept his cabin in the village. His son insisted that he move closer to town, or into one of the comfortable senior citizens apartments, but Vick refused to leave the harbor. "Don't take me to town," pleaded the ninety-one-year-old fisherman during his last winter. "I want to die in the woods."

In March 1985, amid a howling snowstorm, Vick disappeared. Villagers and family searched for three weeks through March storms. One morning, as searchers combed the woods once more, a ray of sun broke through the woods to penetrate the tall hemlocks near Sandstone Falls. The light beamed momentarily on a moss-covered log as a searcher walked down the path. With the sun highlighting the log, the searcher stopped—bits of color in the snow. Next to the log lay Vick, only a half mile from home and his boat, the Nancy Jean.

John Ramsay and his artist wife Nancy evened the population with the birth of their daughter, Macy Anna. They lived on the high banks of the river like the early settlers in the harbor: without electricity or other modern conveniences.

Their wedding on Memorial Day Sunday had been straight out of a storybook. Peggy and Dean surprised the bride and

groom with a black surrey pulled by one of Peggy's horses waiting at their cabin door. Surprised into giggles, the couple
climbed aboard. The wedding party fell in line and followed
them through the village.

Near the water, the bride and groom climbed the path to a
ledge ringed with pots of bright geraniums. Lake Superior waves
pounded out the wedding march on the boulders far below. Fog
lifted as they were pronounced husband and wife.

Changes have come to the harbor. The Sail Inn was destroyed
by fire; there was talk of rebuilding. The Krohns moved on, and
new owners rented the cozy log cabins at the Bear Track Inn.
Come late winter, thawing waterfalls send spray to mix with air
so clear and crisp that it almost intoxicates, and the villagers
listen with hearts throbbing for the magical "Ice out!" call of
spring.

19

THE SEASONS OF INGRID

IF YOU WOULD KNOW Ingrid Bartelli, ride with her through an Upper Peninsula woods, stand beside her under a spreading hemlock at sunset as trout poke ripples in a stream, sit at her favorite window and watch chickadees scatter seeds at her backyard feeders. If you would know Ingrid Bartelli, listen closely as she describes the seasons.

"Spring is soft," she says. "Like pastel colors. Like a warm puddle with mud oozing between your toes. Like a pocketful of fishing worms. Like a newborn child or a lamb or a bird or silk-spun cocoon. Like rain on your face and dew on the grass. Like a birdcall at dawn. I never miss a birdcall. I hear every bird that sings."

When spring's melting snows swell streams to rush madly through the forests, Ingrid ventures over north woods back roads and trails, fishing, walking, searching for Linnaea, "those tiny pink twin-trumpeted blossoms on a fragile vine entwined in the moss on a shaded log, with a powerhouse of fragrance.

"Later in the season, burst a bubble from gum of the balsam

tree for a real reward," she says. "I think every man should smell of balsam."

And the best of Ingrid's world is the beginning of mushroom season, especially morels. Ingrid's name became synonymous with wild mushrooms during her years with the Michigan State University Cooperative Extension. Back in the mid-1950s, after she had begun doing some television shows about food, "people started arriving at my door with bushel baskets of mushrooms, wanting to know which ones were edible." Ingrid found some information available locally, but knew she would have to learn much more about mushrooms to satisfy the growing demand for knowledge. She turned to the University of Michigan and Dr. Alexander Smith, the nation's foremost mycologist. He agreed to help. Smith taught Ingrid, who passed on the information to a thankful public. Ingrid also collected U.P. mushrooms for Dr. Smith. The University of Michigan still maintains the Bartelli collection. "I never got to the state that I was a scientist, but I could sort the edibles from the poisonous," she says.

Ingrid became so well known and sought after that a trip to the grocery store for an orange or two might take several hours, thanks to people who stopped her with questions about mushrooms. A ripple of laughter in the produce department easily led shoppers to the smiling lady with a crown of salt-and-pepper braid circling her head.

As a great many mycology doctoral candidates also turned to Dr. Smith, he arranged summer fieldwork for them, to be completed at Ives Lake in the Huron Mountain Club, near Marquette, under the guidance of Ingrid. "They became my kids," she said. When Dr. Smith visited the camps he was accompanied by wife Helen and daughter Nancy, author of *A Morel Hunter's Companion*.

"Summer is swift," says Ingrid of nature and the outdoors in general. "It's growing and going. It's people and places. It's dew pearls on the grass, a spider's web, spots on a ladybug. Explore it with a berry pail, fish pole, or mushroom basket in hand. Summer is swift." And summer is Ingrid. On the go, with so many things to discover and so many outdoor experiences to savor that twenty-four hours is simply not enough for her day.

138

Outdoors is a way of life for this bubbly lady with the contagious laugh, who now sports a close-cropped hairdo.

Summer lets loose streams, which can "wash all the weariness out of your bones when you wade in it with a fish pole in your hand. Listen to summer," she says thoughtfully. "You will swear an elephant is coming if a porcupine ambles in your direction when you're sleeping on the ground."

Ingrid Mattson Bartelli grew up on a cutover farm in the middle of the woods in Iron County with six brothers and sisters and a widowed mother. "I learned early that nature is bountiful, that nature grows – it heals and gives new life." They lived out of a Sears, Roebuck catalog, "working hard to live and harder to give. Mother was the teacher. No matter how busy she was, if we saw a bird's nest or a flock of geese she would come, even if she was in the middle of baking bread. If we saw a bear in the field, we gathered everyone up and ran after it, in case we could see it again, but of course we never did. I was grown and teaching school when I realized I was still chasing bear."

As the oldest child, Ingrid led the five-mile walk to school in "scratchy knitted underwear pulled down over wool winter stockings to keep our legs from freezing." Finally, during her last year of high school, Ingrid's mother relented to her daughter's pleas and bought her a fancy pair of silk and woolen stockings. It was a bitter cold day, but Ingrid insisted on wearing them anyway. By the time she arrived home, her legs were so swollen and blistered that "they had to start at the top of the stockings and cut them all the way off. Such vanity!" Summers were better, and with the family fed, babies to bed and cows to pasture, Ingrid could "sit on the pasture bars and listen to birds sing and watch the afterglow. I soon learned to go to the out-of-doors for strength and restoration."

Mrs. Mattson was determined that her children work toward a college degree. With a 4-H scholarship in hand Ingrid enrolled at Michigan State University. Because she stayed over to earn an extra thirty-three dollars working at the U.P. State Fair, she was late in arriving for the beginning of the fall semester at Michigan State. A fellow passenger on the train instructed her on getting to the campus and the Home Economics Department. The next morning, Ingrid walked into the dean's office, plopped herself down, and announced, "I'm Ingrid Mattson and here I am!"

When summer break came, Ingrid's family watched closely to see if she had assumed the airs of city life. Headed off for fishing one morning, she met up with her uncle working his daily postal delivery route. Noticing the worms squiggling from a shirt pocket, he was reassured. "I guess college isn't going to spoil you after all," he said.

After graduation, she accepted a teaching position at L'Anse. Soon thereafter she met Leonard Bartelli, a dashing state trooper at the L'Anse post. Her students were not too pleased when Bart married Ingrid and took her away from the classroom. They moved to Marquette, and Bart turned in his troopers uniform to become a state fire marshal so that they could put down roots in the Upper Peninsula for their children, Carolyn, Barry and Barton.

"Fall is full," she says. "Full of harvest, the bounty of the land. When winter approaches, our trees snuggle their feet under the warm comforter of brilliant fall leaves and then a soft downy blanket of snow, trunk and limbs standing bare, watching for spring."

Bart always let Ingrid wander off by herself to the woods, Harlow Creek, or the Yellow Dog River in the evening, kicking up leaves, a fish pole in hand. "Nobody asks why you are there if you have a fish pole. I would throw a line and watch the evening come. I'm a worm plunker. We depended on fish when I was a kid. We only went fishing when the weather was right, and we had to come home with fish."

In his book *Trout Magic*, John Voelker confesses that he never fished with his friend Ingrid. "Yet if she fishes with half the zeal and savvy she brings to our wild mushroom hunts (of which her knowledge is simply awesome), I just know she's got to be a fishing whiz.

"Ingrid belongs here anyway because of deep love of the outdoors and all its lore," he wrote. "Before I got to know her I rather fancied myself as a fairly savvy amateur naturalist, but after a few trips with Lady Ingrid I knew I'd been groping my way through the woods sightless ever since boyhood. She can

141

rattle off the names, both popular and Latin, of all manner of shrubs and herbs and wildflowers and vines and trees and mosses and various fungi, including mushrooms, of course, like kids today can tick off the ten top tunes."

Winter . . . a time for rest, relaxation, rejuvenation, hibernation, a time to restore the soul. Ingrid says winter is watching a gray lake with teeth bared and waves thrashing, bushes bending down in prayer, transformed into snow monsters by a single storm. It is feeling the out-of-doors with your body, flexing your muscles against the blizzard. It is a frost-painted forest on the windowpane framing a visiting winter wren. "It's worth driving across the continent to hear one." She says the outdoors is increasingly important in this "mixed-up world. When the people world gets all mixed-up, we can turn to this other world of the outdoors and restore our equilibrium."

Ingrid says it is time for Nancy Smith Weber and the others to carry on the cause of wild mushrooms. She says there is danger in pursuing the wild and sometimes poisonous edibles past the summertime of life, especially when a misidentification could mean someone's life. "Dr. Smith would be proud of me for letting go," she says. "He said my best attribute was realizing how little I knew."

Part of her is still tied to mushrooms. She still cares. She shows up on field trips "to see my kids," urging for someone in Michigan to teach the basics of mushrooms. "There is little being done about this very valuable resource, while people kill themselves trying."

Now with her braid clipped, Ingrid bakes cookies by the dozens and has become a full-time grandma. She's taken up rockhounding, which she calls her first self-indulgence.

"In contrast to mushrooms, rocks can sit and wait for you, but you can still seek and find. I don't do anything with rocks. I don't make jewelry. I am curious about the stories they have to tell. I have a speaking knowledge of trees, flowers, birds, but I did not know this wonderful, fascinating world of wonder at our feet."

As with mushrooms, she carefully records her findings and

sends the specimens along "to people who know. Maybe it will help someone."

Ingrid's is a good life, surrounded with family and friends, and filled with rockhounding, bird song, and a "lungful of morning air, which erases all yesterday's discouragements and sets the pace for a new and happier day."

20

ISLE ROYALE FISHERMAN

THE FISH HOUSE stands low against the water, silver logs blending into the background of boulders and thick forest of Isle Royale in the western waters of Lake Superior. There is a dock, with weathered skiffs nearby, waiting for repairs. A high wooden rack stands like an upturned landbound windmill, nets that haven't seen use for a dozen years or more wound loosely around the frame. Underfoot, the trail is no longer a natural walkway beaten down by rubber boots of fishermen and their families, but a mixture of small pebbles from a greenstone beach dumped there by the Isle Royale National Park Service.

The odor of trout from the fish-cleaning table permeates the fish house, mixing with the spicy aromas of spruce from the forest and the inland sea washing fresh into Rock Harbor at Greenstone Beach where the Rock Harbor Lighthouse stands guard against the sometimes temperamental moods of Lake Superior. On the breeze is the heady smell of coffee brewing in the summer cottage occupied from May to September by Howard "Bud" Sivertson and wife Jan.

In the stillness of dark nights, or days when fog stalks down the long thin channel of Rock Harbor, ghosts of the past ride on the mist—fishermen at the oars, shipwrecks, tales of Charlie and Angelique Mott who spent one dreadful winter marooned on a nearby island.

Bud hears, and captures these spirits of the past on canvas.

"I am an imitation commercial fisherman," Bud says. He may be the imitation commercial fisherman that he claims, but he is a member of the unusual breed of men who fished Superior's cold waters almost a hundred years ago. He fishes for the National Park Concessions and Rock Harbor Lodge from the restored Edisen Fishery. He also acts as interpreter of the fishing industry, and stores up ideas for his winter paintings.

He is a happy man, a spinner of tales with gray hair blowing in the wind and a wide grin complemented by a low chuckle that sets his shoulders to shaking up and down. The artist, who works in oils and watercolors, interprets history with the brush. In red suspenders, cream-colored shirt, working trousers and fisherman's cap, he looks the part of a man of the inland sea. His grandparents first fished Lake Superior when they landed here from Norway in 1892. The senior Sivertson had four children, all who became involved with fishing, an industry already a hundred years old when he arrived.

Ghostly mist whirls in, glad to reclaim this errant island son even as an imitation fisherman.

Fishing has always drawn people to this forty-five-mile-long island. Low boulders mark the east shore, boulders stained dark by waves and orange lichen, interrupted by stretches of pebbled beaches and occasional strips of sand. Cliffs on the island's western shore are topped with low plants, fans of cedar branches, and sharp spires of spruce pointing to the sky, mixed with toppled trees, which are signatures of the wilderness.

Remnants of prehistoric copper mining pits trace the island's history for centuries. The first white men were the voyageurs who paddled across the expansive sea and past the island in search of furs. They, too, stopped for fish.

"I think they learned to eat from the wolves," Bud says with a laugh. "They could eat a five-pound trout at one sitting."

Isle Royale's glaciated ridge protruding above the waters, one of the oldest in the world, is closer to Minnesota and Wisconsin, but it is claimed by Michigan. It is surrounded by two hundred smaller islands, which provide a natural habitat for fish in the bays and long fingers of peninsulas.

Scandinavian fishermen came. Isle Royale reminded them of their homelands of Norway and Sweden. In their first years of fishing, catch was primarily siskiwit trout.

"When fried, siskiwit end up as no more than skin, backbone and a couple of eyeballs," Bud says. Old-timers rendered them into fat, which they sold to pharmaceutical companies. The oil was also used in the manufacture of paint and other products. Some of the trout were salted for human consumption.

Then came herring, which Bud declares to be one of the finest of fish, and his choice of Lake Superior fish, which he says is "like the taste of pork chops compared to pigs knuckles" of other fish.

"People think of herring as pickled, not realizing how good they can be. Nothing makes a Norwegian happier than to be knee-deep in herring, unless it's being in a candy store with five hundred dollars. And when you get a fresh fish, it's just like eating candy."

Lighthouses already marked the danger spots, including the 1855 Rock Harbor Light near the Edisen Fishery where Bud and Jan spend summers. Until the 1950s, April 1 was the traditional date for fishermen to move back to the island from the mainland. They set hooks and lines "like a long horizontal clothesline suspended under the water for five miles, using herring bait they caught in nets." Wives were up at three A.M. to get their men out the door. The workday for the fishermen was from four A.M. to ten P.M. Bud says they fished in this manner until mid-July, when they switched from hook-line fishing to gill nets on the spawning reefs, until mid-October when the season closed for two or three weeks.

He tells of shipwrecks and fishermen who salvaged what they could from these wrecks, including barrels of flour brought home by his grandfather. Flour and water formed a natural seal on the inside perimeter. His grandmother Sivertson opened the top, scraped away the seal, and dipped into the dry core. "She baked for days," he says with a chuckle.

Four sons followed the senior Sivertson in the pursuit of fish, which had changed in emphasis to whitefish and lake trout. Bud is the next generation, the generation of imitation Isle Royale fishermen who pay their dues to their ancestors who braved the gales and waves by recording this legacy on canvas.

When Bud's grandfather landed on Isle Royale in 1892, fishermen's shacks dotted the bays and coves. Lighthouses stood on rocky outcroppings and islands. Eventually, close to seventy-five commercial fishermen depended on Isle Royale waters for their livelihood. "There were a lot of nooks and crannies for fishermen."

It was a time of moose and a kind of wolves different from the dozen or so that now inhabit the island. Bud recalls Big Jim, the wolf who didn't know what to make of the people moving in with the Park Service in the late 1940s and early 1950s. Wolves started hanging out to beg. "But Big Jim got away," he says with a satisfied grin.

Moose were part of his growing-up years. He says that during fly season, moose would come up to the fishermen's camps to rub and scratch themselves on the walls. "To the moose, the walls acted like sandpaper." About twelve hundred moose now inhabit the island.

Life on the island was simple, with workdays orchestrated by the weather. Daily chores were necessarily performed in a primitive manner. One day, Bud's father decided to provide the family with an unheard-of luxury for Isle Royale. He would build a washing machine!

He filled a barrel with water, and equipped it with an outboard motor from one of his fishing boats. He added soap, dropped in the clothes and started up the motor. On hand to watch the wonderful invention, the family watched open-jawed as their sudsy shirts and pants and aprons and socks sailed past to land on rocks, in trees and everywhere.

At the Johnson fishery, Mr. Johnson's partner Peg Leg Gilbertson enjoyed entertaining the Johnson boys, Alfred and Arnold, when he would get a little drunk. He would have a few snorts, laugh uproariously, and stick his jackknife into his wooden leg. "But he had to give it up when Alfred and Arnold started trying it on themselves," Bud says.

There was excitement in the air when the man from Tiffany's came on the Booth Fisheries boat once a year. He came all the way from New York City to buy greenstones that the fishing families gathered.

Greenstones were polished to a waxy luster, mirrored with grays, tans, whites, and occasionally pinks and reds.

Fishermen Mike Johnson and George Sawyer ground and polished their stones with a grindstone before they got a foot pedal sharpener. Then one of the Johnsons made a polisher from a treadle sewing machine.

They never knew which mail boat the Tiffany man would catch. And even if there was no mail, or groceries, the Tiffany man might be on board. But they didn't have to rush. The skipper was always accommodating. He always waited until someone ran home and gathered up the bag where the greenstones were stored.

It was an exciting time when the big steamships from Detroit and Chicago came into view. They usually anchored off the rocks from the resorts scattered around the island. Somehow the big Indian at Belle Isle knew when to expect them. He could be counted on to climb the high boulder on the point and sit with arms folded as the steamships came into view.

On the rare times fishermen and their families got together, there were days of hard work and hard play. At least once a summer, all the fishing families gathered for a fish bake. The all-day social gatherings were marked with women cooking in the kitchen and men gathered around a roaring beach fire to party and sing sentimental songs about their homeland.

"Men would start out about a hundred feet from the fire, singing their songs and enjoying other entertainment. They would allow plenty of time for the cocktail hour until the women got smart and moved us closer to the fire," Bud says.

Fishermen brought chickens to the island for eggs and for food. Bud tells about cows kept by fishermen in Siskiwit Bay. With no proper landing docks to accommodate cow-sized ferries, cows were made to walk the plank. They were tipped into the lake and herded to shore. When hay got scarce on the rocky mainland, one enterprising fisherman loaded his cow in the skiff and rowed her to a different grazing island every week. "The cow learned the route. She got tired of the skiff, and started swimming to the next island on her own. That cow in the skiff is the subject of my next painting."

Bud was brought to the island at the age of three weeks. Summers were spent in Washington Harbor, where he remembers walking logs across bogs as a child, playing along pebbled beaches, and working on the boats as soon as he could lend strength to pull the nets. The kids created their version of baseball, with the outhouse as first base, the rosebush as second, a corner of the chicken coop for third, and an oar borrowed from the fish house as home plate.

And when the mist rolled in, the kids told ghost stories about Charlie and Angelique Mott who spent a winter on nearby Mott Island in the mid-1800s.

Angelique was tall for a Chippewa, big boned and strong. She wasn't taken in with the men who talked Charlie into staying over on Isle Royale to protect their copper claim while the rest returned to Sault Ste. Marie for supplies. But Charlie insisted. They left La Pointe, Wisconsin, with half a barrel of flour, six pounds of rancid butter, and a few beans, and landed on Isle Royale in early July.

The bateau filled with provisions for the summer never arrived. Summer turned to autumn, then winter. A sudden storm took their boat from which they fished. The day before Christmas, the last of the food was gone.

They had built a shelter and here they waited through the long nights and short days. Wild berries were covered with snow; wild roots were sealed in the frozen ground.

Finally, sick and crazed with fever, Charlie threatened to kill Angelique and eat her. When the fever passed, so did the madness. Finally he died.

In death, Charlie was still a problem. Angelique couldn't bear to leave his body outdoors for animals to eat. She couldn't keep the fire going in their shelter lest he spoil, and she must have fire. Angelique managed to build a second shelter and move the fire. She took comfort in visiting Charlie once in a while.

In later years, Angelique told of the dark times, of trying for days to snare a rabbit with a trap of woven hair torn from her head, and especially of waking in the night with dreams of cutting up Charlie and making soup of him.

Finally, one day in May she heard a gunshot. The promised bateau of provisions had come. When they asked about Charlie, she pointed to the shelter, leaving them to face him alone.

She burned with anger when they searched his body, searching for clues of foul play as though she could ever harm Charlie. They searched his body for violence, but nobody could blame Angelique for her dreams. The awful dreams pursued Angelique for the rest of her life. She found work with a founding family of Marquette. Some nights, they could hear her screaming in her dreams, "I did not eat Charlie, I did not eat Charlie." Sometimes the crashing sounds in the waves beating against the ancient boulders of Mott Island sound as though Angelique were calling still.

When kids grew to "fishing size," they accompanied the fishermen. But Bud's mind wandered; he dreamed of fiery sunsets on canvas and saw a painting in every day. Finally his father would shout for him to quit his dreaming and pay attention to the fish.

Bud says he became an artist in kindergarten. He tells about moving to Duluth to begin his formal education when he was five years old. "The teacher asked us what we did all summer. Other kids talked about baseball games and city buses." Young Bud tried to tell about life on Isle Royale, about playing in bogs, climbing lightstation steps, fishing, searching for greenstones. The teacher didn't understand, and suggested he draw a picture on the board.

"I started drawing and kept drawing until I filled up all the boards. Then she patted me on the head and I was an artist," he says with a chuckle.

He continued to help on the fishing boats, "getting up early with no talent. Then I decided for sure I was going to be an artist."

Pete Edisen was one of the last fishermen on the island. He left the island for the last time in 1977, and died in 1982. Bud loves to tell Pete Edisen stories, especially about the fisherman's legendary tolerance of animals and birds. Bud says sea gulls regularly followed Pete as he went about his chores. "Sea gulls would land on his head and ride along with him wherever he went. Folks asked Pete if it bothered him when they soiled his shirt. He would shrug his shoulders, and say, 'If you want to have good friends, you have to take a bit of that.'"

Bud says he was the next generation that would have fished, "except for the lamprey and the demise of lake trout."

But there is suggestion of more. Bud talks about his twenty-five years as a commercial artist and three years when he decided to "cash it all in and lose myself in the northern woods of Minnesota." He came out with the same dreams he had dreamed on Isle Royale in his youth.

Afterward, he searched for ways to "preserve the character of these colorful independent risk-taking fishermen." Flipping through the family album, he discovered that nobody took pictures of fishermen at work. He began to paint fishing scenes: men in rubber suits leaning to the oars of a homebound skiff, mail boats, voyageurs.

Several years ago, Bud came to Isle Royale and home, called by gossamer mist on the waters, waves that can pound against the boulders to reclaim deeply imbedded greenstones and scatter them along the beach, called by sea gulls floating on the wind, called by two hundred years of commercial fishermen. He and Jan moved into a new cabin behind the restored fishery. Inside the boat house hangs Pete's collection of oars, his motors, fish scales. Bud points to the trap door leading to the water, and the workbench in the back. "This was his workhouse," he says.

Bud busies himself around the fishery, interpreting Isle Royale commercial fishing for visitors in the park, catching his limit of three hundred trout to perform an assessment, recording data for the Michigan Department of Natural Resources.

He waits for the gulls to return and follow him around as they followed Pete Edisen. Meanwhile, he stores up ideas for the next painting dedicated to a disappearing way of life.

21

JUMP RIVER ROSE

WE DRIVE ALONG a dark highway with only the dim lights from the dash, hum of the engine and the beam of the headlights to break the monotony of the night. If I turned my head to the left, I could see the faint silhouette of the man at the wheel. Familiarity allowed for the long stretches of easy silence.

Finally, he spoke in a deep resonant voice. "I was in my midtwenties when I met Jump River Rose. Twenty-five, twenty-seven, maybe, at the age when we didn't care for anything and we thought the whole world revolved around us.

"Jump River Rose was a big woman, close to six feet tall and weighing maybe 165 pounds. Not fat. Well-proportioned because of her height. Not beautiful, but striking like an Amazon princess, striking in a way that made folks turn and stare when she walked past. Her hair was tawny and hung down to her shoulders in a soft billow."

I wondered what dark shadows in the night had prompted this memory, but remained silent.

"She came from down on the Jump River in northern

Wisconsin, and ended up waitressing in a bar in logging country not too far from Lake Superior. Jump River Rose must have been thirty-five or so when I met her. She was something! She talked like a logger, but somehow from her it wasn't offensive. Maybe her size made up for it, I don't know.

"For some reason, she liked me. I used to stop by to see her when I was in that part of the country. We would carry on long conversations about a lot of things. And I suppose you could say we became friends.

"Then Jump River Rose moved on. I didn't see her for quite a while. But one day I stopped in at the bar. Someone said a friend of mine was in the back room. There she was, sitting at a table with two loggers with an arm all bandaged up and her face all bruised. She was glad to see me."

I could tell by the inflection in his voice that he was smiling.

"Despite the bruises, she still looked good. She said she had just gotten out of the hospital with a broken arm. In a burst of her usual colorful language, she told me she had fallen off a 'dumb skidder' in the woods. We visited for a while, and it was almost like old times."

I imagined them there, heads together, laughing easy laughter, catching up on each other's lives. I imagined the years beginning to write its story at the corners of her eyes. I imagined his broad shoulders, sandy hair, which is sandy still, and most of all his steady voice, which echoes of deep forests and rushing north woods streams. I noted how he never said her name without saying it all, like it was a title or something like a cloak that she wore.

"I didn't see Jump River Rose for a long time," he said. "Years passed. Then I heard she had bought a bar in Ladysmith, a little town of less than four thousand people. One day when I was traveling with my partner through that part of the country on a business deal, I suggested that we stop in to see her. We took the two end seats at the bar. A waitress came down, and we ordered coffee.

"I could see Jump River Rose in the dim light down the bar. It must have been more than twenty years since I had seen her, but

I wasn't prepared for this Jump River Rose. Had I met her on the street, I would have never recognized her.

"She was talking to a customer, and I waited. Then she turned my way. She squinted, and I watched her studying me. Even after all those years, she headed straight down the bar in my direction, calling out my name in a questioning tone, loud and brassy, with a hint of the voice I had known."

He was quiet for a while, lost in a flood of memories.

"Life had not been good to Jump River Rose. She was fat. Her face was old. The tawny hair had faded. I should have expected that. She was glad to see me. She tried to act like Jump River Rose, but it wasn't enough. You see, when I had known her, she didn't need to act. She was Jump River Rose."

The car droned on, headlight picking up shadows ahead. Finally he said, "I wish I hadn't stopped. I wish I had left the past alone. I wish I could have kept the memory."